MARCH OR DIE

Moving forward when your world seems out of control

JEREMY M. STALNECKER

MAKING LIFE BETTER
MLB
PUBLISHING

To the men of First Battalion Fifth Marines who taught me how to March when it would have been easier to Die. I am in your debt.

ACKNOWLEDGMENTS

The stories and lessons of this book have been on my heart and mind for a very long time. Rarely does a day pass without at least a short time of reflection on the events contained in this text. It is not an exaggeration to say that I would not be the person that I am today were it not for my service as a United States Marine. That time is something for which I will always be proud. Because this time is so personal, however, and because I have so much respect for the men with whom I served, it has been extremely challenging to get to the place where I am able to tell these stories. Not because they are painful or bring back long buried emotions, but because I don't want to get them wrong. I want the telling of them and the application of "Lessons Learned", to reflect just how deeply I feel and how thankful I am to have been a part. I am grateful for the many people who have encouraged me to share these stories and life lessons despite my own insecurities. Without their help and encouragement, this book would still be a "someday" project.

While it would be impossible to mention everyone by name there are a few that I would like to point out. For my wife Susanne, thank you for your continual encouragement and for reading what I write even when I am sure you would rather do something else. You do it for me and for that I am thankful. For my parents who have been encouraging me for years to write down much of what is contained here. Thank you for patiently listening and reading the very rough early version of the manuscript. Thank you to Chad Robichaux who always motivates me to do more than I would if left to my own devices. Thank you also to John Mizerak and Making Life Better Publishing for keeping me on task and pulling all the production pieces together. To Kate Lehman for your helpful and thoughtful editing and to Barbie Ray for the incredible cover. I could not have done this without each one of you.

Finally, I want to thank the Marines of First Battalion Fifth Marines who taught me so many of the lessons that have shaped my life. There is no way that I could ever repay you. I hope that by sharing some of these lessons our time together can be a help to many outside of our brotherhood.

My desire for this book is to convey the message contained in Philippines 3:13-14:

Brethren, I count not myself to have apprehended: but this one thing I do, forgetting those things which are behind, and reaching forth unto those things which are before, I press toward the mark for the prize of the high calling of God in Christ Jesus. (Philippines 3:13-14)

Thank you.

MARCH OR DIE

ISBN: 978-0-9991821-2-3 March or Die Hardcover

Edited by: Kate Lehman
Cover Design by: Barbie Ray Designs
Published by: Making Life Better Publishing
Learn more information about the author at:
www.mightyoaksprograms.com

TABLE OF CONTENTS

Section 4: Change is Inevitable—Don't Be Surprised When It Happens

Section 5: When You are Stuck, You Only Have Two Options: March or Die

Final Thoughts

PREFACE

Over the last several years I've met men and women from every branch of service who have spent years of their lives deployed to the wars in Iraq and Afghanistan. It's not unusual for those who joined the military around 2001 to spend most of their time in uniform deployed to one of these theatres of war. I have great respect for those who decided to go into the military knowing that they would go to war and then, for many, go back again and again. To these defenders of peace, we owe a debt of gratitude. They are the warrior class that provide the freedoms so many of us enjoy.

My experience as a part of the Global War on Terror was different than many of theirs. I began my journey in the Marine Corps in 1996 when the world, at least the part I cared about, was experiencing relative peace. I deployed for the first time in January of 2001 to Okinawa, Japan, on what amounted to a long training exercise. Nothing very exciting, but it was about the best we could hope for as part of a peace-time Marine Corps. When the events of September 11, 2001 took place, it did not take long to realize that the world had changed. But it did take a while to understand just how much it had changed.

Nothing like this had ever happened, so the road forward was not very clear. I thought that whatever part the Marine Corps would have in this war would be short and involve only a few Marines. Clearly, analyzing world events is not my strength. By the end of 2002

I had submitted my paperwork to leave active duty and had as an End of Active Service (EAS) date July 1, 2003. The war was going on in Afghanistan, and we knew it would eventually make it to Iraq, but our battalion was scheduled to go back to Okinawa and return just in time for me to get out.

I had pointed my entire life toward military service and leading Marines in combat but now believed that it was not meant to be. I had no choice but to accept this and begin to make plans for the next phase of life. And then, for a reason that is still not entirely clear to me, with only a few days until our scheduled deployment, we were sent to Kuwait instead of Okinawa to prepare for the Invasion of Iraq. As I have said before, I am extremely thankful that I had the opportunity to be a part of the Iraq campaign, but I did not go into the Marine Corps or stay in the Marine Corps because I knew that war was imminent and my time there, compared to so many, was short. And yet, those facts being what they are, there is nothing that has impacted my life as profoundly as that experience.

When I finally did leave the Marine Corps, I knew that my time as a Marine and my time in combat were both significant events but believed that I would walk away from them and move on with life. I knew that they would be a part of my life, something I would look back on someday and maybe tell my grandkids about, but I did not fully understand the real impact that they would have on the decisions I have made, the relationships I have developed, and the path of life that I have and am currently living. The Marine Corps and my time in Iraq are not things that I once did; they are an essential part of who I am. I now believe that both were given to me by God to steward for the benefit of others. I know that sounds strange, but I believe that I have a responsibility to leverage my time of service to help others who have served and to communicate the lessons of service to those who have not. And that is the reason for this book.

There are many incredible histories of the war in Iraq, and others have done a great job telling the stories of heroism and personal sacrifice that take place every day in this War on Terror. I am profoundly thankful for both and believe that we need both accurate historical accounts and stories of heroism if we as a nation will continue to appreciate the freedom that cost so many so much.

My goal with this book, however, was different. I did not want to write as a historian, but as a teacher who can take the lessons of history and present them in a way that makes all of us better. To me, this is a part of the stewardship required with a gift like this. To that end, I have attempted to tell stories and then present principles from those stories that will equip us to fight and win the battles of life. It is not just those who wear a uniform who need to know how to fight. All of us will have to fight if we want to live a life of value.

Since the goal of this book is different than other books that deal with war and combat, there are a few things that I would like to point out before beginning. First, I am writing entirely from my personal point of view. I am not attempting to make these stories about me, only to tell them as I remember watching them unfold. The timeline, events and details are as I remember them, and it is not my intention to look over or change any of these. The time that has transpired as well as my admitted failure to always grasp the bigger picture are contributors to any perceived shortcomings. I have intentionally avoided turning this into a research project about the opening months of the war, thus the lack of citations or bibliography.

Second, I have not given the names of the many men I served with in Iraq. Those men are heroes both in the general sense (Americas heroes) and in the personal one (they are my heroes). I look up to them and am proud to be counted among them. I'm still close to several of them and feel that we have a bond that could only have been developed in war. I did not include their names here because I could never in a book like this give them the credit for their actions that they rightfully deserve. I hope that someday that book will be written.

Finally, I am grateful for all who have served and understand that my service was just a very small part of a much larger effort that has involved millions of men and women. I hope to use my experience to help others, and I hope that all who have served will do the same.

I trust that this book will be entertaining and informative, but more than anything I hope that it will be challenging. Wherever you are in your life right now, I pray that the lessons found in these pages will encourage you to press forward and fill you with hope for what is possible.

We are all in a war. The question is, how do we move forward when the world around us is falling apart? Let's figure it out together.

INTRODUCTION

Life is hard. It doesn't matter who you are, where you come from, what you look like, or where you live. If you've been around for more than a day or so, you've experienced something difficult.

Even the process of birth is hard. Both for the mother and the child being born (and the father, I believe, although I may get some pushback on that one), the process of bringing a life into the world is painful and traumatic. Then comes the difficult part—living! Ups and downs, victories and set-backs all blend together over time to make us who we are. And although we would like to think that the good and bad will offset each other, the truth is that sometimes the bad becomes so overwhelming that we can't see the good and would not know how to get to it even if we could.

This is one of the reasons counseling is such a challenge. Over the last several years I have had the opportunity to work with families and individuals who are dealing with a vast array of difficulties, some so overwhelming that the path forward is anything but clear. In the middle of each of these situations the question is always the same: "What do we do now?"

Early in my ministry life, I thought I had to have a clear answer every time someone asked me this question. I needed to be able to lay out a path with simple, achievable steps that would take the person or family overwhelmed by their situation out of the darkness they were experiencing as quickly as possible. It took me longer than it should have to learn that I didn't have to have all the answers, that sometimes the path forward is not clear, and that it's not my job to convince those who are hurting that it is. My job as a counselor, pastor, or friend is to give hope. To help those who are so overwhelmed that they simply want to quit. To tell them that things will get better eventually, but only if they refuse to give up.

I still believe in helping folks understand the steps they need to take to get out of the darkness, but at the moment of crisis, the most important step that anyone can take is the next one. A counselor can act as a guide, but the decision to simply keep moving needs to be made before anything else can happen. This decision will be the difference between victory and defeat in the many battles that each of us will inevitably experience over the course of a lifetime.

It's amazing to me how much of my perspective on life was shaped by my time in the Marine Corps. A relatively short period of time compared to the rest of my life, but it is, in many respects, the lens through which I view the world. Maybe it's because life is often a battle, and it was in the Marine Corps where I learned how to prepare for and defeat the enemy, whoever he may be. Perhaps it's because I was young and learned the lessons of combat and military life at an impressionable age.

Whatever the case, I have a hard time looking at anything without first asking the question, "What did I experience in the Marine Corps that can help me make sense of this?" This question is not necessarily one that I ask consciously, but regardless of the situation I am dealing with, there is always an experience or lesson I learned there that helps me make sense of it. This is never truer than when dealing with the unexpected challenges of life.

I learned in the Marine Corps that training and preparation and good processes are all important, but when the enemy is engaging you, none of those things matter if you are either unable or unwilling to move forward. Before the bigger, more deliberate steps can be taken, it is important to just get up and take the next one. We will get knocked down, ambushed, and overwhelmed by enemy fire, but we do not have to lay there and die. We can, if we decide to, move to a better position and continue the fight from there.

Unfortunately, in combat and in life, the situation can seem so overwhelming that people give up. In combat this can lead to a physical death, and in life it can lead to a spiritual, emotional, or relational death—not for lack of training or preparation, but because the decision was made to give up instead of getting up and taking the next step forward.

This belief, that sometimes the best thing you can do is to simply keep going, is ingrained in military culture. This was one of the first lessons I learned when I became an Infantry Platoon Commander. It did not come from a class or any particular conversation. I didn't learn this life-altering truth because someone taught it to me. I learned it because my Infantry battalion lived it!

In 2000 I checked in as a newly minted Second Lieutenant to the best unit in the military (everyone says that, but in my case, it's true): First Battalion, Fifth Marines. One-Five (or 1/5 as it is known) is a part of the most decorated regiment in the Marine Corps, Fifth Marine Regiment, and has participated in every major conflict in which the

United States has been involved since 1914. That, along with a proven track record of success in those conflicts, makes its motto "Make peace or die" extremely appropriate.

Unit mottos are important in the military because they set the tone and reinforce the culture of the unit. Sometimes they are tied to a historical event, and sometimes they just reflect the general attitude of those who claim it. Either way, the unit motto makes a statement that can be difficult to ignore. I have always liked the 1/5 motto because it doesn't just make a statement; it gives a choice. If you're the enemy, you get to choose: either make peace (on our terms, of course) or die. Pretty simple.

When I checked in to 1/5 on that June morning in 2000, I was assigned to be a platoon commander in "C" (Charlie) company. The companies in a battalion, for those not familiar with Marine Corps organization, are the smaller units that together make up the battalion. What's funny about Infantry companies is that, even though they are all part of the same battalion, they each believe they are the best part of that battalion. So each company develops their own identity, complete with logos and mottos, so that everyone else knows they are the best. Oddly enough, this whole system works. And the motto of my new company?

"March or die."

What a great motto! It says as a company we're just going to keep moving forward, and we are going to do so because the alternative is death! There is no going back and no stopping. When we don't know what to do, we will just take the next step.

Over the years I have been asked several times by people outside the military how service members can do some of the amazing things they do in such difficult situations. While I'm sure that there are many answers to that question, one answer is that they don't have any other choice. If they don't do these amazing things, they don't come home. Understanding that there's no alternative to action makes the decision to act easy.

And that is what I have always loved about the Charlie company motto. It's not a statement to the enemy; it's a statement to the Marines. It is a simple way to communicate that the only alternative to forward motion—moving forward even when things seem overwhelming—is death. It really clears things up!

It's been a long time since I was a part of First Battalion Fifth Marines and even longer since I was a part of Charlie Company. I've learned and experienced so many things that have shaped the way I look at the world and the way I look at overcoming the difficulties of life that often seem unbearable. But I would still sum up my thoughts on trial and loss with that simple phrase: March or die.

We complicate life and allow ourselves to become overwhelmed by the trouble it brings, but moving forward really isn't that complicated. It is the process of putting one foot in front of the other, one day at a time. It is understanding that as bad as things seem now, the alternative to pushing forward is death. Not death in the physical sense (although that can sometimes be a consequence), but in the relational, emotional, or spiritual sense.

Simply drawing breath does not make one alive. Living takes place when we decide to invest our energy, our time, and our resources in people and purposes outside of our day-to-day survival. Life happens when we decide, despite history or present circumstances, that we are going to march forward, one deliberate step after another.

Life can be extremely difficult, but the reality is that it is extremely difficult for everyone! So what's the difference between those who overcome difficulty and those who do not? The ones who overcome realize that there is no alternative. They either move beyond the trials and difficulties or resign themselves to simply counting the days until they leave this earth.

My goal for this book is very simple: To give hope. To illustrate through my experiences of the war in Iraq and through the experience of a character in the Bible how to move forward when we don't know what to do. I want to outline steps that can take you from where you are to where you want to be and need to be. The next step is not always easy or clear, but the alternative to taking it is to stay in place and die.

Are you simply going through the motions, or are you living a life of meaning and purpose? Have you allowed your past failures or your current difficult situation to keep you from truly living? It is time to understand that there are only two choices in life: March or die. The next step may not be easy, but it is the most important step you will ever take.

This book was written to not only help you take that next step, but to keep you marching in spite of what the life in front of you may bring. We can't possibly know all the battles we'll face, but we can be prepared when they come. I want to provide both the motivation and instruction you need to make sure you are ready. Each section of the book is a step that you need to take and is broken into two main parts: an event I experienced while serving in Iraq—the motivation—and an example from the life a Bible character named Caleb of the right way to apply this motivation—instruction. My prayer is that as you work through each of these sections you will gain the tools you need to keep moving forward when your world seems out of control. But before we start, it is important that we get the right perspective.

Section 1:

THE RIGHT
PERSPECTIVE

CHAPTER 1 - MARCH OR DIE

I'm always interested in hearing about the defining moments in people's lives, the moments that had a significant impact on them and in some way shaped how they look at the world. These could be tragic events, such as the death of a loved one, or important victories in sports, school, or work. Defining moments are not necessarily the most significant events, just the ones that, for some reason, impacted them more significantly than others.

For me, one of these life-defining events took place on April 1, 2003 at a small bridge over the aptly named Saddam Canal.

By April 1 our battalion had been traveling toward Baghdad for almost two weeks. There is a major highway that extends north from the Kuwaiti border, and we were doing our best to move up this road as quickly as possible. At the time it felt like all we were doing was driving, but, in retrospect, we made relatively little progress. It was like a really long, really slow road trip with a thousand friends who were quickly getting tired of each other. Only without the snacks and energy drinks. There was a lot of dirt, too, and we had to sleep sitting up in our Humvee, so there was that.

Apart from the opening days of the war, we did not experience much that could be called combat. There were a few skirmishes here and there, along with a pretty significant sand storm, but for the most part we drove and we waited (which is probably why everyone was getting tired of each other). It's funny how quickly things can change.

During the morning commanders' brief we were given the task of securing a small bridge traversing one of the many canals in Southern Iraq. Not surprisingly, the canal was, like so many things in this country, named after the dictator we were trying to remove. Our mission was to get to the bridge and set up a secure checkpoint so that another battalion could cross while continuing north. The intelligence we received indicated that there were no enemy troops there, so we would set up our checkpoint in the middle of the day because it was unguarded. It was always better to deal with the enemy at night when we had the advantage, but it was definitely easier to move during the day, particularly when there weren't any threats.

Hindsight is twenty-twenty, as they say, but it should've seemed odd that the division was sending a battalion of Marines to secure a small, unguarded bridge. But for some reason, attacking an unguarded bridge in the middle of the day with 1,200 Marines made perfect sense at the time.

As our battalion pushed toward the objective my platoon took its normal place in the column. Not only did we navigate for those coming behind us, but our vehicles also provided forward security since we had heavy machine guns. Bravo Company was behind us and would be the main effort in setting up the checkpoint. Our job was to get to the bridge safely and get out of the way so they could go to work. Simple enough, and something we had trained to do many times before.

German military strategist Helmuth Von Moltke famously said, "No plan survives contact with the enemy," and ours definitely did not. The ground and road leading up to the bridge were flat and free of any vegetation and reminded me of the fields in California where I grew up just after they were prepared to be planted. The clear, flat ground and the late afternoon sun allowed us to see the objective from a distance of what seemed like a few miles. In reality it was probably less than a mile (memory tends to distort distance), and as soon as we hit the straight section of road that led onto the bridge, the artillery rounds began to fall. This "unguarded" objective had a battery of D-30 artillery pieces firing 122mm artillery shells on top of our road.

I will never forget the taste and smell of the smoke as those rounds narrowly missed us. I knew that the battalion had artillery available to us but was out of radio range to do the necessary coordination. We worked to relay messages back to our Fire Support Center, but we were in a spot where there was nowhere to take cover, and the enemy was actively engaging us.

We did our best to continue pushing toward the bridge to get into position, but it didn't take long for us to figure out that the artillery was not the only thing waiting for us. Dug into the side of the hill facing us was a company-sized element of Saddam's Republican Guard (the guys I had been hearing about since the Gulf War twelve years earlier). We found out the size and origin of the unit later, but the threat they posed to us and the other Marines in the battalion was immediately clear.

We now had a second severe threat that we hadn't anticipated and that could, if not dealt with, be fatal.

UNDERSTAND THAT THE BIGGEST FIGHTS IN LIFE COME WHEN WE LEAST EXPECT THEM.

Because of my own life experiences and listening to others talk about theirs, I've realized that the next battle always seems to pop up seemingly out of nowhere, when things are going well. All the intelligence tells us that everything is fine and will continue to be for the foreseeable future. But then something happens. A financial reversal, the loss of a loved one, or an unfavorable doctor's visit—all situations that we didn't see coming—throw us into a tailspin from which we struggle to recover.

Understanding that these fights will come is important. Not so that we can live life scared or overwhelmed with anxiety about the future, but so that we are prepared when the unexpected happens. I have met and talked to so many people who have given up in life because a battle came that they didn't expect. They have been hurt, but instead of dealing with the hurt and working to make the situation better, they become life-long victims of a one-time event. Because they did not expect the problem, they allowed it to overwhelm and sideline them when it did come.

Others allow the unexpected battles of life to drive them into a deep state of introspection. They freeze as they try to figure out what they did wrong to deserve their current circumstances. While it's true that sometimes we end up in the middle of something hard because we made a bad decision, it is also possible to do everything right and still have artillery rounds dropped on us.

When you find yourself in an unexpected fight, change any bad behavior that may have gotten you there and then stop trying to figure it all out. You have a fight in front of you, and worrying about how you got there will only get you killed.

YOU MAY NOT BE ABLE TO CHOOSE THE FIGHT, BUT YOU CAN ALWAYS CHOOSE HOW YOU FIGHT.

When we finally made it to the enemy soldiers who were using everything they had to kill us, we did exactly what we were trained to do. We overwhelmed them with the necessary force to ensure that we would win the battle. We had trained in peace so that when a situation like this one popped up unexpectedly, we would respond quickly and accurately. Which we did.

There is an ancient proverb (I don't actually know how ancient or how proverbial, but it is a good saying) that says, "The more we bleed in peace, the less we bleed in war." Often, even though we did not choose the fight or the battle, we can still come out on top if we are prepared. Although I was never a Boy Scout, I have always liked their motto, "Always be prepared." While I'm sure it's impossible to be prepared for *everything* we might encounter, we need to live with a preparedness mindset. Always learning and growing so that when we do deal with the unexpected, we will at least know where to begin. When we drift through life unprepared for the difficult times that we'll inevitably face, we may not die physically (as in war), but we will die emotionally and spiritually.

You may not get to pick the fight, but decide before the fight comes to you that you will not let it keep you down and that you will do everything you can to win. There are so many people who live their lives just getting by, which keeps them one bad event away from a major failure.

We may not get to choose the fight, but if we prepare before it comes—and it will—then we can choose how we fight. The enemy is waiting; we need to get ready.

CHANGE IS INEVITABLE—DON'T BE SURPRISED WHEN IT HAPPENS.

As the battle unfolded, it quickly became apparent that the original plan of staying on the near side of the bridge was not the best course of action. As we worked to figure out how to deal with the incoming artillery, a new threat presented itself. Our enemy had set up an anti-aircraft gun on top of the bridge as a measure to keep helicopters from flying over. It decided that at the moment, we were more of a threat than aircraft.

The gun was probably no more than fifty yards away and intent on keeping us off of the bridge. Even though we were trained to deal with many different types of enemy weapons, never once did we talk about how to deal with an anti-aircraft gun rotating all four barrels in our direction. I had been confident up until that moment that not being a pilot would keep me out of a scenario like this one.

The situation had changed, and it had changed quickly. Apparently the enemy was allowed to adjust our plan, and even though our mission was to stop just short of the bridge, we pushed all the way to the top so that we could deal with this new threat.

I made some mistakes that day that I'm sure put the platoon in a more dangerous situation than was necessary. One thing we did not do, however, was stop and talk about how the situation was changing and that the enemy was not playing along with our plan. We were able to adjust as circumstances changed because changing circumstances, although they did cause some friction, did not surprise us.

It's amazing how well you're able to deal with a changing situation when you don't allow it to surprise you. It has been said that the only constant is change, and this is certainly true in combat. Thankfully, because of quick action and accurate fire, we were able to take the anti-aircraft gun out of commission.

So here is the question: How many times have you put a plan together meant to deal with a difficult situation and then something changed? You decided that you were going to deal with the battle in front of you, but your plan began to fall apart, and when it did, so did you! So much emotional energy is required to even decide to fight (particularly when you didn't choose the fight, when it's not your fault) that when circumstances change we become too overwhelmed to go on. Most of us like to have control, and a loss of control damages our pride and drains away whatever motivation we had. This is why relationships that once appeared to be strong begin to disintegrate after a family tragedy or financial difficulty. A loss of control due to a changing situation begins to erode our motivation to continue on in other important areas of life. We did not expect things to change, so we weren't prepared when they did.

Just as the battles come when we least expect them, so does change. Build change into your plan, and then when it happens you won't be knocked off guard! Do your best to move forward with the information available to you, but be ready to adjust the plan when the circumstances surrounding you shift. Whether in combat or life, it is those who know how to quickly deal with change who will come out on the other side victorious.

WHEN YOU ARE STUCK, YOU ONLY HAVE TWO OPTIONS: MARCH OR DIE.

Getting on top of the bridge to deal with the anti-aircraft gun was a good move. Staying there was not. In the heat of the battle I managed to get eight of my vehicles into a very small space that made us a big target. In fact, the D30 artillery battery must have planned for this because the artillery rounds quickly began to fall around us. It's a miracle that no one was killed while we sat there.

We quickly understood that the top of the bridge was a target that our enemy had previously established and that we were in the aptly named "kill zone." As I stood outside my vehicle trying to direct the fight on the radio, a round fell so close that the explosion sent a shockwave through my body. I can almost feel it even now as I think back on that moment. It was how I imagine running full-speed into a wall feels like, only I didn't fall.

The smoke was so thick around us that I thought one of the rounds had blown up a vehicle. Another explosion caused one of our section leaders to fly off his feet and land on his back. We were in a bad situation that was quickly getting worse.

I wouldn't have been able to say it exactly like this as it was happening, but my platoon was stuck in a spot with only two options: Stay where we were and die or move to a better fighting position. This is where our training and preparation kicked in. The leaders in the platoon intuitively understood that we needed to move and, almost in unison, we did. We quickly moved off the top of the bridge and finished the fight in a place where we could win. When caught in a bad situation we knew, just as I had learned a few years before in Charlie company, that we either needed to march or die!

Here is the point: When you find yourself stuck, whether in a place of your choosing or not, you only have two choices. You can either choose to stay where you are and die, or you can get up and march to a place where you will be able to win the fight.

It's remarkable how many people who find themselves in a bad situation simply lay there and die instead of getting up and taking the steps necessary to move beyond their situation. It may not be a physical death, but it is an emotional or spiritual death that may, in fact, be worse.

Breathing and working a job and making others think that you have it all together is not the same as living. Living is getting up every day and taking the steps that need to be taken to fulfill the purpose for which you were created. Allowing an unexpected battle to keep you from moving forward is making the decision to die.

The decision to march, however, is refusing to let your circumstances, whether present or past, define your present or your future. Marching, just like life, takes place one step at a time! You may not have all the answers, but you make the best decisions you can with the information you have and take the next step you know you should take. It's amazing what will happen when you simply decide that you are not going to quit. Although your trials may be complex, your options in the middle of those trials are simple: March forward one step at a time or stay where you are and die.

BAD DECISIONS DO NOT NEED TO BE FATAL.

We often find ourselves in a battle because of the bad decisions we've made. Disintegrating relationships, financial challenges and a lack of direction can be imposed on us, but more often they are the result of things we've done. We look around for someone to blame for the circumstances of our life, but the only ones we can honestly blame are ourselves. This can be an overwhelming realization that can cause us to quit instead of motivating us to get up and make a change. Instead of marching forward, we stay where we are because it's our fault, after all.

The goal is not perfection but persistence. The only one who can disqualify you from living a life of value and purpose is you. So often we disqualify ourselves when, really, we just need to take the next step.

As this engagement with the enemy came to an end I remember experiencing an overwhelming peace along with the thought that it just doesn't matter. It does not matter who you are or where you came from or even what qualifies you to be here. The best you can do is the best that you can do, even in the worst situations. You are not responsible for anything outside of your control, but you must do your very best to control the things you can.

Combat, physical or otherwise, does not care who you are. Take the pressure off yourself, stop disqualifying yourself because of something that you have done or something that has been done to you, and put one foot in front of the other. You need to march so that you will not die. The goal is not perfection. It's persistence.

CONCLUSION

We make life so complicated when, really, it's pretty simple. Even though we may find ourselves in complex situations, the decision we need to make in the middle of them is not. Whether the battle is one of our own making or one that was forced on us by someone or something else, we need to decide that instead of giving up and staying where we will die an emotional and spiritual death, we are going to march forward one deliberate step at a time. The choice is and will always be yours.

So what are you going to do? Will you march or will you die? The time to decide is now!

MARCH OR DIE.

- *Understand that the biggest fights in your life come when you least expect them.*
- *You may not always be able to pick the fight, but you can always pick how you fight.*
- *Change is inevitable—don't be surprised when it happens.*
- *When you are stuck, you only have two options: March or die.*

CHAPTER 2 - THE DECISION MAKER

My goal in the next several chapters is to use real events from my life to equip you to continue marching forward when life is a little, or even a lot, out of control. We cannot keep the difficult things in life from happening to us, but we can decide that when they do, we will push forward.

And that is an essential element of success in this area. We must decide. As I illustrate the steps that need to be taken to move us forward, I understand we can know what we are supposed to do, but still fail to do it. And we fail, not for lack of knowledge, but for lack of a decision that leads to action.

I grew up with parents and mentors who consistently showed me the right steps to take in life, so when I do fail, it is rarely because I didn't know what to do. When I fail in my personal life or family life or in my relationship with God, it's usually because I decide not to take the steps I know I should take.

People who successfully deal with trial and difficulty are people who have decided that they will continue to move forward with God's plan for their lives regardless of what happens to them or around them. They decide before the difficulties arise that they will not quit.

To help us see the power of decision in action, I will end each section with a story from the life of a Bible character named Caleb.

Caleb was a remarkable man in a number of important ways, but a key to his success was his ability to decide to move forward when the world around him was falling apart. There were moments in his journey when he could have quit, and no one would have blamed him for doing so. But because he decided, again and again, to take the next step, he moved beyond the difficulties—hiking through the desert for forty years and watching most of his friends die—and experienced incredible victory. As we close out each section Caleb will show us what it looks like to put the steps we know to take into action. Let's get some perspective on Caleb's life, and then we will jump into our first step.

CALEB: THE DECISION MAKER

Imagine being chosen for a special mission initiated by God Himself. After waiting for the fulfillment of a promise made by God to the nation of Israel, that's exactly what happened! Following the well-known Exodus from the land of Egypt that included ten incredible plagues and the parting of the Red Sea, God led Israel to the edge of the Promised Land. This was the land that God had promised to give them as a place to settle, raise families and worship Him. It was the place that they had prayed for, dreamed about, and now were finally getting ready to occupy.

Before they went in, though, God told their leader Moses to do something interesting. In the Old Testament book of Numbers chapter 13, God told Moses to pick one man from each of the twelve tribes of Israel to go into the land as spies. Their mission was to see firsthand everything that was waiting for them so that they could come back and give a report to the rest of the people. God wanted the spies to tell the others what a wonderful place this new home was so that they would be excited for the next step in their journey. The Bible passage is specific when it tells us that these spies were not just any men, but leaders in their respective tribes. They were men of influence who could mobilize the people for the work in front of them.

One of the spies chosen was a man named Caleb. We are not told much about Caleb at the beginning of this story other than he was a member of the tribe of Judah and he was forty years old. He was also a warrior and a leader and had faith in God, but at this point in the story all those things remain to be seen.

Caleb must have been excited and thankful for the opportunity to represent his tribe on such an important mission. I am sure that life felt very good as the pieces began to come together for the future for which he had been hoping.

And then, to make things even better, the land they saw was beyond anything they had imagined. They described this new territory as a "land flowing with milk and honey" (Numbers 13:27) and told the rest of Israel that they had never seen anything like it! They even brought back samples of the fruit and other crops stretched between two poles so that everyone else could see it for themselves. The heart of Caleb must have been full of joy and tremendous hope for himself, his family, and his nation as he considered just how blessed they were by God.

But even though all was as God said it would be, ten of the twelve spies did not give a positive, hope-filled report to the rest of the nation. Despite the beauty and provision of the land, these men were scared because of the people who lived there and the battles that would need to be fought before they could occupy it. These leaders of the tribes of Israel did not mobilize the people for the work in front of them but filled them with fear by convincing them that they were in great danger.

Caleb and one other spy named Joshua (Moses' right-hand man and eventually the leader of Israel) could not understand how, after everything they had seen God do up to this point and after spending time in the land that He had promised them, the spies could possibly bring such a negative—the Bible calls it "evil"—report. They had everything going for them but watched it all slip away because a few men allowed themselves to become overwhelmed by fear instead of filled with and motivated by faith.

The negative words of these ten men had such an impact on the rest of the nation that they began to cry out to God, weeping all night and saying things like, "We would have been better as slaves in Egypt than dying here in the desert." This was their go-to accusation: We would have been better as slaves than in this difficult place where all we can do is trust God. They went so far as to accuse their leaders of being at fault for the whole thing!

Finally, in Numbers 13-14, the people stopped talking and God started. This fascinating conversation between God and Moses ended with God giving His judgment. You really need to read it for yourself in Numbers 14, but the abridged version is this:

God told Moses that because of the people's rejection He was going to wipe them out and start over. He told Moses that He would grow Moses and his family into a great nation so that He would no longer have to deal with the crying, complaining and rejection. Moses responded by giving the reasons that God should not destroy Israel and begged Him to continue the work that He had started.

God listened to Moses' defense of the people and told him that even though He would not destroy them, there would be a consequence for their unbelief. No one in the nation of Israel over the age of twenty (except for Moses, Joshua, and Caleb) would be able see or enter into the Promised Land. The Israelites would wander around the desert until everyone who was above that age died, and only those who were now young people would be able to go forward. This decree from God began a forty-year period where the people traveled through the desert without a home, waiting for the day they would finally be able to occupy what God had promised.

This story illustrates so much of life. Everything is going well, and the pieces are beginning to line up. Just like Caleb we find ourselves in an enviable position, in a great relationship or job or something else that is important to us, and it feels like life could not get any better. We may not be where we want to be, but we are quickly on our way. A few good decisions and a couple of well-placed steps, and we will get there.

But then everything changes. We feel like the rug is pulled out from underneath us, and we are left alone and confused. The change often isn't because we have made a bad decision, but because someone else has. We lose a relationship or a job or some level of security because someone else in our life made a decision that negatively impacted us and those around us. And just like Caleb, we see hope and promise slip away.

The truth is, even though our story may never be as dramatic as that of the nation of Israel, we all know what it's like to move from hope and promise to frustration and confusion. Life can be so overwhelming that just about the time we think we have it figured out, it spins out of control again.

Unfortunately, that is just life and living. What we learn from this story (and many like it) is that these turns of event or out-of-control moments are not the end. There is still victory to be found if we are unwilling to allow the things that happen to us to define us.

Often we decide to give up when we are overwhelmed or we feel like our future was somehow taken away. We will do the minimum that is required of us from now on and just get by. The problem is that "getting by" is not living. It is breathing and existing, but it is not living.

One of the fascinating things about this story is that after Caleb makes an impassioned plea to the people to pursue God's promise, he stops talking. At least as far as the Bible is concerned. I have a picture in my mind that once he had said everything he could say and heard the judgment of God, he went home and got the family ready for a long journey through the desert. And in case you're wondering, he came out on the other side and finally received all that God had promised. He made a decision that he was not going to let his circumstances or the decisions of others to keep him from moving forward.

Whatever you're dealing with right now, don't give up. I know that it might be bad, but it's probably not *wander around in the desert until everyone you know is dead* bad. Don't allow yourself to get so caught up in what is happening to you that you take your eyes off a God that promises to "never leave thee nor forsake thee" (Heb. 13:5).

Life may be confusing and out of control right now, but when you don't know what to do, do the best you can to prepare for whatever lies ahead. Decide that even though this is not how you had envisioned it, you are going to keep pressing forward toward the life that you have been promised.

You don't have to understand. You don't have to be in control. You don't even have to be the one who is responsible for where you currently find yourself. You do, however, need to decide to get up and take the next step.

The story of your life may look bleak at times, as it did for the nation of Israel, but God is not done working. Don't give up before He has time to do all that He has planned.

Section 2:

UNDERSTAND THAT THE BIGGEST FIGHTS IN YOUR LIFE COME WHEN YOU LEAST EXPECT THEM

CHAPTER 3 - NOTHING EVER GOES AS EXPECTED

As one might imagine, the days leading up to the push from Kuwait into Iraq were a strange combination of long hours of waiting mixed with long hours of preparing. When we weren't waiting, we were preparing gear and vehicles and making sure our weapons were ready to go. And then we rehearsed. Over and over again we rehearsed in order to be as prepared as possible for the opening hours of the war.

For those not in the military the idea of rehearsing for a combat operation may sound strange, but we wanted to remove the variables, or as many as possible, that could be the difference between success and failure. These rehearsals took different forms, from large, division-size briefings on a giant terrain model laid out on the ground to smaller platoon level map surveys. The goal was to ensure that every person involved, from the Division Commander to the newest private, would know exactly what they were supposed to be doing every minute of the opening battle of the war.

One of the most often rehearsed aspects of the plan was how each unit would link up with other units fighting in the same space. It would become necessary as the battle progressed for these connections to be made. But without a clear process of identification and communication, the chaos of the battlefield could make this very difficult. We had to get this part of the plan right.

Believing that our initial attack across the border would take place during the first light of the morning, our signals for link-up were all visual. Large markings on the sides of vehicles would identify each unit so that when a link-up became necessary, it would be easy to see who was who. Lanes of travel would also be designated with visual markers so that we would be careful not to drive into the minefield that would be set before our arrival. This was a complicated operation, but our comfort level increased as the plan was rehearsed and discussed until we could recite each step clearly and with full understanding.

By the early evening of March 18, 2003, we were all ready to go the next morning. Everything was in place, and we were sitting just a few miles south of the Iraqi border in the Kuwaiti desert. As a final measure of preparation our battalion commander, Lt. Col. Fred Padilla, had each of the unit leaders gather for one final briefing.

While he stood and briefed us on the timeline for the next several hours, a Marine who had been monitoring the radios interrupted and handed him a note. After reading the note Col. Padilla looked up and said simply, "The plan has changed; we are going now." He then looked at the Chaplain and asked him to say a prayer before we went back to get our Marines on the road. When "amen" was said at the end of the prayer, we ran back to where our companies and platoons were set up and began the movement toward the border.

IT IS THE UNKNOWN OR UNEXPECTED THAT GETS US. SIMPLE THINGS DESTROY THOSE WHO CAN'T ADJUST.

Since we were making our movement toward the border and ultimately to our first objective several hours early, what was supposed to happen in the light of the morning was now happening in the dark of night. Since so much of our plan was based on being able to see the other vehicles on the battlefield, it was clear that this was going to cause a problem.

I wasn't consulted before changing the start time of our

movement, but I was told that one of the reasons we were moving earlier than planned was because some of the oil lines that ran across our objective had been broken and set on fire, and we needed to get to them before they were beyond repair. This complicated matters further, since now, with all the smoke in the air, we could not even use our night vision equipment to see. We figured it out, but what was supposed to be a simple, straightforward attack was made extremely complicated because of a slight adjustment in the plan.

The first several hours after crossing the border into Iraq were probably the most stressful of my life (and others as well, I'm sure). We knew the plan for that attack so well that any Marine in our battalion could have stated clearly what he needed to be doing at each stage of the plan's execution. When the plan changed, though, we had to adjust so that we could still accomplish the mission. We kept the parts that weren't affected by the changes, but our ability to maneuver and connect with others at pre-determined link-up points became extremely difficult.

It's a funny thing about plans: they rarely go the way you think they will. You may have it all figured out and even be able to picture in your mind each of the pieces coming together. You move forward believing that nothing could knock you off course. But then circumstances change, and you find yourself adjusting to a situation that you could not have anticipated.

It's amazing how many people simply give up when what they thought was going to happen didn't. A job or a marriage or a path of life just didn't work out the way they thought it would, so they quit. It is always the small, unforeseen obstacles that get us. In many ways, the ability of an individual or an organization to adjust to changing situations will be the key indicator of their success.

You need to plan so that you can reduce as many of the variables as possible, but don't become so tied to your plan that you can't change. You will need to. Be ready.

NOTHING GOES AS EXPECTED. WE GET ANGRY BECAUSE WE WANT TO BE IN CONTROL.

Over the next few days the situation was constantly changing. We had hundreds of Iraqi soldiers surrendering to us, others trying to fight, and an oil pipeline on fire. To add to the friction, we had prepped the area before arriving with small bomblets dropped out of a plane. These acted as land-mines on the ground around our objectives. This made travel very difficult since we were constantly trying to avoid them.

On the second day of the war the vehicle that I was traveling in ran into one of these "friendly" mines and blew out all four tires, destroyed the fuel lines and vehicle undercarriage, and would have killed everyone inside if we had not taken the precaution of sitting on sandbags! These were the early days of the war before armored undercarriages became standard. The shrapnel that came up through the floorboard punctured the sandbags, and no one was hit. Amazingly, a piece of shrapnel did come through next to the gas pedal, where we couldn't put a sandbag, but missed the driver and everyone inside the Humvee on its way out through the roof.

Even with all the damage done we managed to keep that vehicle on the road all the way to Baghdad and back to Kuwait. Our mechanic used some JB Weld to patch up the holes, and we were good to go. We did have to use jet fuel dumped into the exhaust to get it started, but somehow it all worked.

These factors (everyone was dealing with something similar) along with a few days without sleep caused the frustration levels to rise and the anger levels to rise with them. It is crazy how angry we can become when we lose control of a situation unfolding around us. When we lose control, we look for someone or something to blame, whether they are at fault or not. This emotional outburst then becomes the reason we can't take the steps necessary to get back on track. We are so busy finding fault that we don't have the ability to find a solution and can, if we're not careful, damage relationships with the very people who can help us find that solution.

Instead of getting angry when we lose control, we need to control the things that we can and stop worrying about the rest. Finding or assigning fault is only helpful when it moves us towards a solution and never helpful when it is simply a way to absolve ourselves of responsibility.

As situations change and control is lost, focus more closely on the things that you can affect and begin looking for new ways to move forward. Anger can lead to a loss of control. Blame is never helpful. Find new ways to accomplish your mission.

BAD THINGS HAPPEN. RESPOND APPROPRIATELY AND THEN KEEP MOVING FORWARD.

That first morning in Iraq something happened that we had often talked about and planned for but never really believed would happen.

The first KIA of the war in Iraq was Lt. Shane Childres. Shane was leading his platoon in clearing a small group of buildings when they got into a firefight and he was mortally wounded.

This was a surreal moment for many because even though we knew this could happen and did happen in war, it just didn't seem like it would happen this way. Shane was a great Marine who had spent time enlisted before becoming an officer and Platoon Commander. He was extremely professional and very likable, someone you just enjoyed being around. When I first heard on the radio that he had been shot, it never crossed my mind that he would die. He even called in his own medevac!

When word spread that he didn't make it, the reality of our situation finally set in. This was not a training exercise. I will never forget the meeting that our Battalion CO had with the staff and officers the next day. I think for many of us, the expectation was that he would share some words of wisdom and we would have a prayer or moment of silence. I didn't know exactly what would be appropriate in that situation, but I knew he would.

The meeting was short, only long enough for him to reflect on what we had just been through the previous few days and then to give the orders for us to continue forward. Before he did that, though, he addressed the issue on all of our minds. He started by mentioning our casualties, both wounded and killed, and then reminded us that there would be a time to mourn but that this was not that time. He immediately turned our attention back to the task at hand and sent us off to accomplish the next mission.

It was difficult to process, but I walked away feeling like I had been told that the loss we had experienced was unimportant. Some of these men, like Shane, were friends, but all were brothers in arms. It took me many months to understand what had happened during this short meeting. It may have seemed unkind at the time, but what had actually taken place was that our CO taught us an amazing leadership lesson. I have reflected on this lesson hundreds of times since then and have used it to deal with other times of difficult loss.

The lesson we were taught that day was both simple and profound. As we move through life bad things will happen. Relationships will be broken, people we care about will be lost, and circumstances will move in an unexpected direction. There will be, and should be, a time to mourn the loss or adjust to the change. But life cannot stop.

Just as our Battalion CO had to lead his battalion forward in the midst of tragedy, so we must lead those around us when things are dark. Don't allow what has happened to define you or to keep you from moving forward.

We did have a time to appropriately mourn the loss that was experienced that day and in the days ahead. And so should you. And then it is time to get on the road again. Bad things happen. Respond appropriately and then keep moving forward.

CONCLUSION

That old phrase "Expect the unexpected" is more than just a quaint saying. When we understand that nothing ever goes exactly as planned, we won't be knocked off course when our situation does change. We need to control what we can and plan to eliminate as many variables as possible.

There are times when the failure of a plan is nothing more than a failure to actually plan. We have an idea of what we want to accomplish but never do the hard work of figuring out what is needed to succeed. There are those who live their lives by winging it and then wonder why they accomplish little of significance.

The success that we experienced during the opening days of the war was because of our plan, not in spite of it. While it's true that much of the plan changed, we were able to deal with the parts that did because we were still in control of the parts that did not. We need to plan. We just can't feel bad when the plan doesn't work out.

Many people have stopped really living because something that they planned for never came together. They stop trying to achieve because the last time they worked hard, the result was different than they expected. They no longer dream because their dreams have never become a reality.

But the purpose of planning is not perfection. The purpose of planning is to provide enough margin that when things do not work out exactly as planned, adjustments can be made and the mission can still be accomplished. A plan that changes is not a failure—it is the next step toward success. Whether you take that step, though, is up to you.

Accept change as a part of life. Plan and work and then be ready to adjust. How you deal with change will largely determine your success or failure. Plan to change, and you will plan to succeed.

NOTHING EVER GOES AS EXPECTED.

- *It is the unknown or unexpected that gets us. Simple things destroy those who can't adjust.*
- *Nothing goes as expected. We get angry because we want to be in control.*
- *Bad things happen. Respond appropriately and then keep moving forward.*

CHAPTER 4 - IT'S NOT ABOUT YOU

One struggle we all have in common is a difficulty looking at the world from a perspective other than our own. We tend to look at the events in our life as impacting primarily us, and we determine whether something is good or bad by the impact it has on us. This is why it's hard for us to imagine that others are suffering when we have our needs met or get angry when others enjoy their lives while we struggle. When we forget that the world doesn't revolve around us and that we are just one of 7 billion people on this planet, we lose the ability to see our struggles as they really are. We lose the proper perspective, which can lead to a loss of hope and direction.

One of the best things that we can do for ourselves as well as others is take a step back when we're overwhelmed and look at life from the vantage point of others. This allows us to get the right perspective on what is actually happening and helps us to see the way forward.

This is another lesson that I learned looking back on my experience in Iraq; it was completely lost on me while events were unfolding. Involvement in war is a good excuse to be selfish, and I embraced that excuse with both arms. I have often thought that I missed much of what could have been learned (both at home and in Iraq) because I was so focused on my well-being and viewing all of life from wherever I happened to be standing. I'm not sure that hindsight is always

20/20, but I do know that looking back has helped me to learn some of the lessons that I missed the first time. I guess we can even learn when we do things wrong!

WHEN WE FOCUS ON OTHERS, EVERYTHING CHANGES.

During the time I was in Iraq my two oldest children were three and four. My wife was taking care of them by herself while also dealing with the many administrative issues of life. When people outside of the military think of those serving, consideration is rarely given to the spouses who are left behind. I believe that we should express our thanks to the men and women who fight to keep us safe, but we should also thank the husbands and wives who make it possible.

I know that not every military family situation is ideal, but I also know there are thousands of families doing well because of a spouse who holds it all together. I wish I had worked harder to understand what my family was dealing with. I knew what I was involved in and how it was affecting me, but I often forgot the impact that being away from my family was having on them.

We forget that when any family member is going through a difficult time, the whole family is affected. We don't live in isolation and must consider the impact our actions have on the ones we love. When we look at our situation from the vantage point of others, we learn that we are not alone and that life is bigger than what we are dealing with right now.

It's easy to say things like, "No one understands what I am dealing with. No one knows what it's like to be me." It's only a blinding focus on self that prevents us from seeing how the things we are dealing with impact those who care about us. We do not live in isolation, and we do not struggle in isolation.

If we look beyond our own struggles and understand how those struggles are affecting others, we find the motivation we need to get up and move forward. When we begin to understand that it's not all about us, we begin to see the world, or at least our part of it, as it really is.

During my deployment, my wife would send me letters and pictures of the kids and do her best to keep me informed and encouraged. This was, as one might imagine, very important to me. But in an extremely self-centered way, I felt like I deserved it. I was doing something important in a foreign country far from home while she and the kids were living their lives in the middle of a middle-class American neighborhood. Instead of trying to understand what they were going through and doing what I could to encourage them, I waited for them to encourage me. There were a few things I was overlooking when I considered their situation:

1. I had chosen the life of an Infantryman, not them. They did not decide to be a part of a family that would include long periods of time away from husband and father, along with the worry and responsibility that goes along with having a deployed family member. I was doing exactly what I had chosen to do and worked hard to do, but they had to adjust their "normal lives" to make up for the void that I was intentionally leaving. They may have been more comfortable physically than I was, but in a very real way they had little control over their lives or future. They

had to respond to the decisions that I made and the good or bad that came as a result.

2. Even though I was involved in a major military conflict, I had very little to worry about outside of the mission. I rarely thought about where I was going to sleep, what I was going to eat, or how my finances were going to work out. None of these things may have been exactly what I would've liked them to be, but they were not on my list of concerns for the day. I was 100% focused on the job at hand. For my wife, however, that was not the case. We had moved out of our home shortly before I deployed, and she was living at her parents' house while trying to find a home for us to purchase. She was taking care of two small children, managing our finances, and putting the pieces in place for our family life after the military, all while worrying about whether I would be a part of that "life after the military." I knew what was happening in Iraq all the time, but she knew only what she could piece together from news clips and articles. I never worried about the safety of my family while I was away, but when the news reported that a Lieutenant from our battalion had been killed without releasing the name, she had to wait for several days before she knew whether it was me.

3. As chaotic as it could be at times, my job was something I had practiced for, an extension of training that I had done thousands of times before. For my family, each day presented a new set of challenges that they weren't prepared for and hadn't yet thought

about, and they would have to figure those challenges out as they came up. I'm not suggesting that war doesn't have its own unique fears, concerns, and stress—it does. The difference is that I chose that life and prepared for it, but my family just had to deal with it.

And all of this while still trying to be an encouragement to me. In hindsight, I can only imagine how different my perspective on the events of that time would have been if I had just tried to focus on others instead of focusing only on myself and what I was dealing with. I can't know for sure, but I imagine that if I had been more focused on others, I would have:

1. Sent more letters to more people instead of wondering every day why I didn't get more. I'm sure that even with the right perspective I would have loved to get mail (which I did), but working to encourage others while I was away would have included others in what I was doing instead of making them the cheerleaders and me the player.

   I was blessed to get mail from my wife and kids, my family and friends as well as many people I didn't know who simply wanted to be encouraging. By taking my eyes off of myself for a few minutes, I could have used a very unique opportunity to cheer on those who were fighting their own difficult fights.

2. Done a better job communicating to those who cared about me why I felt it was important for me to be a part of what was happening there. Since I believed I was the only person in my family who'd be affected by this trip to the Middle East, I made no attempt to express how I felt about it. When asked what I thought about the war by those I cared about, I would tell them that it was my responsibility as a Marine to go. That was my equivalent to pushing away those in my life who wanted to help me and wanted to understand for their own emotional well-being.

Going to war was something that I had always wanted to do. Not for the war part, though. For me it was about being a part of something bigger than myself and putting to the test the years of training leading up to that point. I have always looked up to leaders, and this was my chance to see if I could lead in that environment. This was not something that I dreaded but something that I looked forward to and felt prepared for.

But I never shared any of that. So when I left, anyone who wanted to be a part of what I was doing and wanted to understand how it was impacting me had to guess. They had to guess and hope that I was somehow prepared for what I was about to face. They had to hope that I had confidence in my leaders and the other Marines I'd be fighting alongside. They had to wonder how I was dealing with this emotionally and if I was scared or excited.

If I had been honest about what this coming event meant to me, I could have removed so much of their anxiety and worry and allowed them to be happy for me instead of scared about how I would handle it. But I didn't. Because at that moment, at least in my mind, it was about me and had very little to do with anyone else.

3. Taken care of all the "other" stuff. Looking back, I realize how much I left for others to take care of while I took care of myself. It may not have been quite that simple, but I could have done more to help those I was leaving behind prepare for my deployment as much as I prepared the Marines I was deploying with.

I emptied our house and locked all our earthly possessions in a storage unit just days before I got on a plane and left the country. This meant that my wife needed to figure out how to take care of two kids in someone else's house, her parents needed to make accommodations for them to move in, and she would need to find a house for us to live in when I returned and start the process of buying. Besides family, there were friends who helped with all that needed to be done, and not one time did I hear anyone complain. I am thankful for the people who are willing to help when others go forward in defense of their country, but I could have made it so much easier.

When we view the events of life only from the perspective of what we are dealing with right now, it is easy for us to drop all the other important details and justify doing so because of what we are dealing with. We all need help, but we need to be very careful not to walk away from the responsibilities we have the ability to fulfill by pushing them off on others.

DON'T MAKE THIS ABOUT YOU. DO WHAT YOU DO FOR OTHERS.

Before the war I believed that the only reason the American military deploys around the world is to defend the ideals and way of life of the American people. Politics aside, most of us can agree that the freedoms long enjoyed by Americans are freedoms that have been paid for by the toil and blood of the American military. For military members there is a comfort that comes from this truth that allows us to believe that we do what we do as a service to others.

As thankful as I am for the opportunity to have been a part of the defense of the American way of life, what I learned in Iraq was that service to others can extend beyond simply serving those who come from the same country as you. When you understand that you are fighting for others, the hardship and sacrifice has value that it wouldn't otherwise.

The rhetoric leading up to the invasion of Iraq, at least as I understood it, centered on two points: the possession of Weapons of Mass Destruction (WMD) and the damage that a decentralized Middle East would have on our own national interests. What I do not remember hearing much about was the widespread oppression of the Iraqi people. As we traveled north toward Baghdad, we would meet wonderful people who were displaced because of the decisions of a government that operated with complete disregard for its citizens. We learned of torture, murder and widespread oppression perpetrated by those who should have been providing stability and safety. There were many examples of this, but one made a particularly strong impression on me.

In an attempt to let the Iraqi people know that our presence was for their good and not harm, we used every opportunity to extend good will by handing out food, making repairs to schools and other public buildings, and removing any munitions that had inadvertently landed on the property of one of the many farms that lined the highway.

One day, as we worked with a local farmer to clear some mines from his field, he began to explain to us why his fields had nothing growing in them even though they had been prepared for planting. He said that even though there was more than enough water to grow food for his family on his land, the government had taken all the water and was making the farmers pay for it. Water from their own wells on their own land could not be used until they paid a fee to the government. The only way these farmers could make money, however, was by growing and selling crops. Without the water they could not grow the crops to make the money to buy the water to sell the crops! And so this farmer had scraped together just enough food to keep his family alive for a few years, hoping that something would change. He was so grateful that we were there and hoped that now he would finally be able to farm his land.

It's not a very dramatic war story, but in a way it changed my outlook on what we were trying to accomplish there. We were, of course, fighting to preserve the American way of life, but in those moments we were also fighting to free innocent men, women, and children from a dictator who was stealing their way of life.

The lesson here is one that I revisit often. We will all, from time to time, find ourselves fighting battles that we just don't understand. At those times we try to justify what we are going through in broad terms—we are fighting for our family or for our future. But even if those reasons are true, they can get lost in the day-to-day grind. It's helpful to look around and understand that there are real people who need us to fight and win the battles in which we are engaged right now. How we end up in the fight is often much less important than who we can help if we will just realize that it's not about us!

Talking with the farmer that day, I realized that one of the things that makes America great is that we have always been willing to stand up for those who can't stand up for themselves. I believe that what makes an individual great is the exact same thing. When we are willing to stand up for those who cannot stand up for themselves and fight and win the battles of life because of those who *need* us to win them, we too are great, if only in the eyes of those for whom we fight.

CONCLUSION

It's not about you. We live in a culture so focused on self that we make everything about us! We can't eat or spend time with our families without telling other people because we believe, even if we don't say it, that we are the reason for everything!

As I write this chapter we are just finishing up the Thanksgiving holiday and getting ready for Christmas. Each of these holidays is supposed to be an opportunity to express thanks and acknowledge that the world is bigger than any one person. If there is a singular example of how self-centered thinking has permeated our culture, though, we find it between these two days of thanks, beginning with the aptly named "Black Friday." One day after Thanksgiving—just a few hours for many—the day of expressing thanks to God and others as we begin a season of "peace on Earth, good will toward men," shoppers maul each other at the store so they can get discounted electronics! The internet is full of videos (often entertaining, by the way) of people being trampled or physically assaulting their fellow shoppers so that they can get a good deal.

Watching this unfold on the news or social media can be entertaining, but it is a sad commentary on a completely self-absorbed society. You and I may not ever be caught on video in the mad rush of Black Friday, but how often do we live our lives this way? We manipulate those around us to get what we want and then feel bad when things don't work out, with little thought for how others may be affected. We are not always self-focused, but our primary concern is our own welfare. Life is about us.

While there are many problems with this self-focus, one of the big ones is the harm it creates in moments of difficulty and crisis. If we believe that the world revolves around us, then we also must believe that the battles we fight do as well. We feel needlessly alone and miss the many lessons that hardship and difficulty can teach. We miss the unique opportunity to be a blessing to others when we focus only on our well-being. And in the process, we destroy relationships, hurt people who care about us, and fail to stand up for those who have no one else to turn to. No one likes hardship or difficulty, but when it comes—and it will—we need to look outside of ourselves and understand the real reason that we fight. It's not about you!

IT'S NOT ABOUT YOU.

- *When we focus on others, everything changes.*
- *Don't make this about you. Do what you do for others.*

CHAPTER 5 - DECIDE: NOT TO BE DEFINED BY YOUR SITUATION.

It's all good until it isn't. It is amazing how quickly life can go from good to bad. One minute you feel like things could not possibly get any better, and the next you are convinced that they could not possibly get any worse. Oddly, it never seems to work the other way around!

This is exactly how events played out in the life of Caleb. He may have actually set a record for the fastest move from on top of the world to wandering in the desert lost and confused. To really understand this, though, we need to get the whole picture.

The nation of Israel began living in Egypt some four hundred years before the Exodus as nothing more than a large family in need of a permanent home. Following a series of unusual events, this family finally did find a home in the country of Egypt (the full story is found in Genesis 37-50). Even though the older siblings of this family sold their younger brother Joseph into slavery, he managed to work his way up to the second highest position of leadership in the country and eventually invited his family to come and live with him. Even though Joseph's brothers intended to harm him, God used the circumstances in his life to protect them! At a time when the world was thrust into a famine, Joseph was able to take care of his family. This story is an amazing picture of how God provides in the worst of situations.

One thing was always clear, though, even as this family settled into a comfortable new living situation: God had promised them a country of their own someday. Egypt was never meant to be their final stop, just a place where they could grow from the family of Israel to the nation of Israel. This was so clear that Joseph asked that his bones be taken with the rest of the nation when they finally went to the place God had set aside for them (Genesis 50:24-26). From the very beginning, they were looking forward to occupying their own country.

As time passed and Joseph and his immediate family passed away, the nation of Israel did grow. They grew so much, in fact, that the Egyptians put them to work as slaves. What started as a safe place to live and grow became a prison due to fear and misunderstanding. As this difficult period stretched on (Israel spent four hundred years in Egypt), many began to lose any hope of deliverance and thought that perhaps the promise of a new country was simply a myth.

I think most of us can relate to this in some way. When we are faced with a difficulty or trial we hang on to the hope of deliverance. Time, however, is no friend to the person who is struggling. The longer a difficult situation goes on, the easier it is to lose hope. If we aren't careful, it's easy to decide that everything we once believed about God and his ability to deliver was nothing more than a myth. Some made-up story designed to give false hope to those who don't know better.

This is exactly what happened to Israel. They had a promise, but with that promise unfulfilled, it became harder and harder to believe. And then everything changed.

God spoke to a man who would become the deliverer of the nation of Israel (the book of Exodus has this story). Moses, a man with a somewhat sordid past, was chosen to lead Israel out of Egypt and into the land of promise. Against all odds, and with the help of a series of plagues that encouraged the Egyptians to get rid of the Israelites, they finally broke free. After four-hundred years of bondage they were beginning to see God's work unfold. This miracle was the fulfillment of generations of promise and prayers for deliverance.

And then, to make things even better, twelve leaders were chosen to go and look at this new land and come back to report on the amazing place that everyone could look forward to (Numbers 13). They were told to report on the people who inhabited the land, the produce that was grown there, and its potential as a new home for Israel.

Caleb, chosen to be one of these spies, must have been overwhelmed with gratitude for the fulfilled promises of God and excited for the next step on this incredible journey. I can just see Caleb as he looked at this new land, envisioning himself moving there with his family. We know from the end of this story that he had already picked out the place he wanted to live. He probably even talked with his family about where each of them would build their houses and looked forward to the days when they could share time together on their own property. He must have felt like he was on top of the world.

But circumstances changed again. When it seemed like all was finally coming together as they had prayed so long that it would, Israel took a turn away from God that would lead them to a generation of wandering in the desert without a home of their own. The report from the spies was intended to encourage the people for the days ahead, but ten of these men convinced the nation that they would never be able to move into this new land. Even though they saw the produce and must have understood the potential, they allowed a fear of the people who were there to overwhelm them. Even though they had seen God work in situations much worse than this one, they did not want to move forward.

To me, this is one of the craziest parts of the story. They had already experienced the plagues in Egypt, allowed God to lead them with a cloud during the day and fire at night, and crossed the Red Sea! But they were still afraid. Fear rarely makes sense but can be so strong that it will keep us from moving forward even though we know we should.

Caleb, along with Joshua, tried to get everyone back on track, but it was too late. The people quickly rejected God and His leading into the Promised Land, and as a result wandered around in the desert for forty years before they finally went in. The other ten spies were killed, and every person twenty years old and older died during their desert march. They stood on the threshold of their promise but walked away because of fear.

I can't imagine what it must have been like to be Caleb at that moment. He must have stood, at least for a minute, in astonishment as these events unfolded. He was one of only two men who encouraged Israel to go forward because he trusted God and His word. But it didn't matter. Caleb was at one of those times in life when, despite the best plan and the pieces of that plan coming together, the end was not what he expected. The outcome wasn't his fault, but there wasn't anything he could do to change it either.

The Bible does not give us much detail about Caleb. We know that he was a leader in the tribe of Judah, that he had a family and children, and that, when Israel finally did go into the land of promise, he was there to take what he had decided was his forty-five years earlier.

While we may not have more details about his life than that, so much can be learned simply by how he handled this reversal in his life.

The same can be said for us. Our truest qualities, who we really are, are revealed more clearly when things do not work out than when they do. We may not have all the details of Caleb's life, but what we do know is that he made a decision before all of this unfolded that he was going to do right and follow God *in spite* of his circumstances. The contrast between him and the other spies helps us see this. When the other spies were looking at the land to determine if they could follow God's plan, Caleb was looking at the land knowing that he would. That's why he was excited and they were scared. He had already decided.

This is the key to moving forward when your circumstances change. When events unfold differently than you had hoped and the pieces that you have worked so hard to put together seem to be falling apart, you will either stay where you are, wandering around in a desert of hopelessness, or push confidently forward.

Caleb was the same man in the desert as he was before it because his circumstances did not define him. But we often allow our circumstances to determine our happiness, fulfillment, and life's direction instead of simply revealing who we have already determined to be. The decision to move forward regardless of what may come your way is the most important decision you will ever make. If you wait to decide until you get a good look at the battle ahead, you will make the wrong decision.

Caleb was not the only man who had determined to follow God's plan. There was another spy, Joshua, who pleaded with the people to trust God and move forward. Joshua eventually became the leader of

Israel and would encourage the people, many years later, to decide to trust God. As their leader he stood in front of them and did his best to help them prepare for the times when things would not go according to their plan. He said this in Joshua 24:15: "Choose you this day whom you will serve." A simple statement, but a statement, when accompanied with action, that will make all the difference.

Choose. Decide. Determine. Don't let your circumstances become your destination. The road ahead may get dark. Things will not always work out as you have planned. Keep going. Remember why you started in the first place and you will eventually, as did Caleb, find yourself on the other side of the seemingly overwhelming trial. It all comes down to a choice.

Section 3:

YOU MAY NOT ALWAYS BE ABLE TO PICK THE FIGHT, BUT YOU CAN ALWAYS PICK HOW YOU FIGHT.

CHAPTER 6 - SOMETIMES YOU MUST HANG ON

In life as well as combat, preparation may be the difference between success and failure. The more prepared we are, the more we can reduce the variables, those unplanned events that have the potential to destroy us. There will always be events that take place completely out of our control, no matter how much we plan.

One such unplanned event took place as we made our way north in the days following the opening push of the war. A sandstorm so large that for a full day combat on both sides of the line came to a halt.

I had heard about the massive sandstorms that would regularly move through this region of the Middle East but was not prepared for just how all-encompassing they could be. While we were waiting in Kuwait a few weeks earlier we experienced a storm that knocked over tents and brought visibility to nearly zero, but it only lasted for a few hours. This time, though, the storm started slowly and grew to the point that we could not even move for fear of veering off course or running someone over.

We had a Marine from an adjacent unit come knocking on the door of our vehicle in the middle of the night because he could not see to get back to his own Humvee. He took just a few steps away from his vehicle to relieve himself and could not see to get back. He stayed with us until the storm blew over.

At night the sky was completely black, but during the day it looked like a scene out of a movie about the end of the world. The light that did make its way through the blowing dirt turned the sky red and made you feel like you were operating on Mars instead of in Iraq. Finally, the order was given to just hold in place and wait until the world got back to normal.

As we were holding and waiting, there was very little thought given to the enemy. We maintained security the best we could, but we all assumed that the bad guys were dug in somewhere as well. That is the odd thing about storms: They are indiscriminate. They effect everyone.

STORMS COME TO EVERYONE, EVEN THOUGH WE FEEL ALONE IN THEM.

As we sat in the dark listening to the wind blow around us, it was very easy to feel alone. Since you can't see anyone else, your mind tells you that you are the only one dealing with the noise and the dirt and the inability to make forward progress. You know that none of those things are true, but your emotions often cloud your better judgment.

Storms work this way in life as well. Something blows into our lives that we did not plan for and have no control over and throws us off course, even if only for a short time. We must deal with the wind and the dirt and the lack of progress that cause us to feel as though we may never get back on track. In the middle of it all, because these unexpected storms are loud and dark and overwhelming, we begin to believe that we are the only one dealing with it. We forget that storms, although they may not affect each one of us the same, do affect us all.

We are not alone in dealing with the impact of this unexpected event. Our family, friends, and others close to us deal with the fallout of watching someone they care for struggle, even if they aren't directly impacted. You are not, no matter how you feel, ever alone in the storm. And in a strange way, knowing this can bring comfort and allow us to look up long enough to help others get through it, too.

SOMETIMES IN THE STORM, THE ONLY THING YOU CAN DO IS HANG ON AND WAIT FOR IT TO BLOW OVER. WE WANT TO DO SOMETHING, BUT GOD SAYS TO BE STILL.

As the minutes turned into hours, what began as confusion and a mad dash to find a secure place to set in became boredom that eventually turned into a growing uneasiness about not doing anything. We had been pushing hard for several days and still had a lot to do before getting to our destination of Baghdad. Sitting still, even during an event as large and out of control as this one just didn't feel right. Once, in the middle of the night, I decided I couldn't just sit anymore and left my vehicle to check on the other Marines in the platoon. Unfortunately, I didn't get very far before I had to go back. There was nothing I could do but sit and wait. Except for one fight that I am aware of, the entire platoon made it through the night without incident even though I was stranded in my HMMWV.

This is one of the most difficult lessons to learn and apply when life takes a turn or a storm rolls in that we didn't expect. The need to be in control, to always be doing something, is strong in most of us. Add to our need to be in control a culture that expects us to be available at all hours of the day, and sitting still while we wait for the storm to pass is nearly impossible.

This is one of the great lessons that storms can teach us, though. When the world around us is out of control, it's time for us to turn our eyes to the One who is bigger than the storm. It is during these times that God is most glorified in us because our full faith and hope for the future is in Him.

In Psalm 46:10 God says, "Be still, and know that I am God: I will be exalted among the heathen, I will be exalted in the earth." When the storm is raging, it is time for us to "be still" long enough to remember that He is God and we are not.

THE STORM WILL ALWAYS PASS.

Why is it that we lose hope in the middle of the storm? There's probably a list of reasons that we could give for allowing the storms of life to overwhelm us, but I believe that the main reason is that at a heart level, we do not believe the storm will ever end. We can deal with just about anything no matter how bad it might be if we know it will eventually come to an end. Knowing when it will end is even better.

For the last few years I have been trying my hand at Brazilian Jiu Jitsu (BJJ). BJJ, for those who are not familiar, is a ground-based martial art that has a lot in common with wrestling. The major difference—and there are many—is that in BJJ the goal is to subdue your opponent, not by a pin, but by choking them or manipulating a joint until he either quits (called tapping out) or is physically unable to continue.

At my age, the learning curve is pretty steep, and I spend most classes just trying to get through. Since all four of my kids are also training, I need to learn as much as I can for self-defense reasons, which makes quitting out of the question. I keep going and trying to learn while also trying to get to the other side of each class with the ability to walk to my car on my own.

One thing that helps me make it through each class, as funny as it may sound, is the clock. Where I train there is a clock over the door that gives the time and another clock on an adjacent wall that counts down when we are practicing, which consists of six-minute rounds of live sparring. When I look at the clock over the door, I know exactly how many minutes are left before the class is over. During those moments when I am not quite sure I want to have someone practice one more choke on me, I can look up at the clock and know—be infused with hope—that this will all come to an end very soon. That is often enough to allow me to re-focus on learning and practice.

The other clock, the countdown timer, is also important. When we are sparring for a six-minute round, I can tell how much time is left, which allows me to know when to take it easy and when to expend my remaining store of energy. Knowing there is an end makes all the difference.

Unfortunately, most of life's storms do not have a count-down timer that tells us exactly when it will be over. Once in a while at the end of a Jiu Jitsu class the instructor will throw an extra round of sparring in even though the class should be finished. As you can imagine, there is a bit of a muted groan across the room as the clock starts counting down once again. But I have never seen anyone get that far in a class and walk out just because an extra round was added. The time-line has become a bit more unpredictable, but there is no question that the class *will* end. Just not when we thought it would.

That's how life's storms can be. We think we know how long they will last, but something changes, and they keep going even though we thought we would be in the car driving home by now. We don't know when they will end, but we do know that they *will* end.

I love the Old Testament story of Shadrach, Meshach and Abednego found in Daniel 3. The order was given that everyone in Babylon would bow down and worship their king Nebuchadnezzar. The problem was that these three men were Jewish and had determined that they would worship only God. As one might imagine, the king who thought he was God did not appreciate their rebellion and gave them a choice: bow down or be thrown to their death in a fiery furnace.

This was certainly an unexpected storm in the lives of these three men that had no clear end. Amazingly, they never lost hope. I am sure they were afraid and had no desire to die prematurely, but they clearly understood that this event was not about them. That nothing lasts forever and that God, if they allowed Him to, would use this event for His glory.

Daniel 3:16-17 tells us how their conversation with the king went: "Shadrach, Meshach, and Abednego, answered and said to the king, 'O Nebuchadnezzar, we are not careful to answer thee in this matter. If it be so, our God whom we serve is able to deliver us from the burning fiery furnace, and he will deliver us out of thine hand, O king.'" These men knew, one way or another that this storm would pass. God would either deliver them from the fire or give them the courage to endure it, but either way the storm would come to an end. And it did! I encourage you to read the story for yourself. This storm may have ended dramatically, but it did end.

I'm not saying that when you are in the storm you should look forward to death as the only way of getting through it. What I am saying is that, one way or another, all storms do come to an end. Your job is not to figure out when or how they end. Your job is to remain faithful, trusting God while they are raging around you.

Storms can bring both pain and an overwhelming uncertainty, but don't lose hope! Do what you know is right, control what you can control, and believe that this storm, like all storms, will end exactly when it is supposed to. Psalm 30:5 says it like this: "Weeping may endure for a night, but joy comes in the morning."

CONCLUSION

Sometimes the most difficult thing we can do when our world feels like it is spinning out of control is nothing. We want to be in control. We want to make the pain and the heartache stop. We want everything to get back to "normal" and forget that any of this ever happened. Often, though, the most important thing that we can do is simply hang on. Do what we can do but stop worrying about the things we can't. Trust the God who is bigger than it all and learn the lessons He is trying to teach us. Do what we know is right, in spite of the circumstances, and maintain hope that eventually this storm will pass.

So many people do things in the middle of storms that they would never do at another time of their life. They end up hurting people and making decisions that will have an impact long after the storm has passed. Hang on, and you will come out on the other side better, not worse, for the storm in your life.

SOMETIMES YOU MUST HANG ON.

- *Storms come to everyone even though we feel alone in them.*
- *Sometimes in the storm, the only thing you can do is hang on and wait for it to blow over. We want to do something, but God says to be still.*
- *The storm will always pass.*

CHAPTER 7 - EMBRACE THE MOMENT

I have always been a goal-oriented person. Not always in the *set a goal, get it done* sense, but in the *get this over with so that I can get back to the couch* sense. The admonition to enjoy the journey is something that I have always struggled with. For most of my life the journey has just been the necessary path to get from where I am to whatever is coming next. When traveling, I just want to get there. While in school, I just wanted to get to the next level or graduate. Each week I just want to get to Friday. When I am doing something difficult, I usually get through it by picturing the ride home or the time in front of the television when it's over.

While this is a solid technique for dealing with difficult situations, it can be a sad way to live. This is exactly how you set yourself up for a midlife crisis or an end of life depression. You accomplish things and move through life but enjoy very little. I honestly believe that this is the reason so many people leave a job or relationship and find themselves empty and lonely.

Accomplishment is not the same thing as living a life of value. With kids, ministry, and the many other relationships in life, it is so easy to mistake the extraordinary events as ordinary or unimportant until it is too late. Not every moment can be enjoyed, but every moment can (and should) be appreciated. How often do we fail to realize just how important a moment is until it and the lessons we could have learned are over?

As a twenty-six-year-old Marine Lieutenant preparing for a major military invasion in a country I had only heard about on the news, my mission was clear: lead my marines well and come home to my wife and kids. This was a moment for which I had spent most of my life preparing. As a fourteen-year-old teenager I voiced for the first time my intention to be a Marine. I remember telling my dad that I wanted to enlist and him telling me that I needed to go to college first. I did, but then had the privilege of going through a Marine commissioning program that allowed me to attend Officer Candidates School after my first year of college. I spent the next few years of college working toward the day I would finally be commissioned as a Second Lieutenant. Again, as was my custom, I spent most of those college years looking forward to them being over. And then they were.

Shortly after graduation my wife and I moved to Quantico, Virginia so that I could attend the Basic Officer Course for new officers where I spent six months learning the skills necessary, at least administratively, to lead Marines. The next school was the Infantry Officers Course, and I spent ten more weeks in Quantico, this time learning how to be an Infantry platoon commander. From there we moved to Camp Pendleton in Southern California, where I became a Rifle Platoon Commander in Charlie Company, First Battalion, Fifth Marines.

There are many people who never get to live out their childhood dreams, but I am not one of them. This was the only thing I had ever wanted to do, and I was finally doing it. A dream that had started to develop when I was an adolescent was finally becoming a reality. Now it was my job to prepare young men to fight our country's battles if the call ever came. We trained, and we worked, and we deployed, all so that we would be ready when America needed us. I know those last few sentences may sound a little dramatic to some, but to those who serve, they are a reality.

And then an event that none of us could have predicted began to unfold. On September 11, 2001 terrorists attacked and killed nearly three thousand Americans in coordinated attacks in New York, Washington D.C., and Pennsylvania. I was on the rifle range when we received word of these attacks, but without all the information, I assumed it was over since the terrorists were dead. Nothing like this had ever happened, and for some reason I didn't think the change in the country and the military would be as profound as it has been.

It did not take long, however, before the reality of those events set in. Training took on a new urgency as we got ready for imminent deployment to the Middle East. And then we went. We loaded planes at March Air Force Base in California and headed for the desert of Kuwait before pushing into Iraq.

Finally we were there. I was getting ready to do what I had guided my entire life toward. Somehow, though, the magnitude of the event was lost on me. The men and women who fight our wars possess something that allows them to do the job they need to do without necessarily understanding why they are doing it. For those in uniform, understanding why is often an unattainable luxury. They simply need to fulfill the mission given them by their commander-in-chief.

Sitting in Kuwait with my division, waiting for the call to

overthrow the dictator in the country just north of us, I was more than happy to follow orders without attempting to grasp the magnitude of all that we were getting ready to do. One of the major regrets of my life is that I didn't even try to understand during this time. It is amazing what we can miss when our goal is simply to get to the other side.

The significance of a major military force moving beyond the Tigris and Euphrates rivers and securing a foothold in the capital city of perhaps the oldest civilization in the world cannot be overstated. Iraq is a country of real historical significance and has rightly been called the birthplace of civilization. It is here where the ancient city of Babylon rests and where the major civilizations and religions of the world began.

Beyond those small but important facts is the reality that the country of Iraq has been at war almost non-stop since it was organized as a sovereign nation. For many generations other nations have laid claim to Iraq and its people, but none have been able to successfully govern it. This is a country of good people who have learned from thousands of years of oppression to simply get by regardless of who may currently occupy the seat of power. What an incredible opportunity to learn lessons and have experiences that could enrich my life and help me view the world in a more meaningful way. But during this experience, I was just happy to be moving closer every day to getting home.

Thankfully, not all the lessons that were to be learned during that time were lost on me. I have had the opportunity to reflect on so many of those experiences, and I believe my life and my outlook on life are richer and more meaningful because of them. However, I do regret that I didn't embrace the moment when it was happening. I regret not learning more or seeing more or having more conversations with the folks who live there. As a student of the Bible I had the opportunity to appreciate much of what I had read about in the Old Testament but largely failed to do so. The experience was not wasted, but it was not all that it could have been.

And so it is in life. We find ourselves in a difficult situation that we know we need to work through and may have even prepared for, but our focus is on simply surviving, not learning and growing. We count the days until it's over or daydream about getting to the other side. Meanwhile, we are missing the fullness of the moment, neither appreciating all that we should or learning all that we can. Life can be extremely difficult, and not every situation or relationship or job will be enjoyed. But every situation can be appreciated when we realize that we are little more than the experiences we have had and the decisions we have made.

A relatively new phrase has begun to circulate in the veteran community that I think sums this up. In response to those who like to talk about post-traumatic stress disorder (PTSD) while emphasizing the disorder, veterans have started using the phrase "Post-Traumatic Growth" to describe what happens after combat. This phrase, taken from a speech by Secretary of Defense James Mattis, is a simple way to explain that our experiences, even when traumatic, do not cause us to become disordered if we will stop long enough to learn from them.

When we begin living to learn and grow through every event or situation, good or bad, our entire outlook changes. We move from simply trying to get by to being grateful for an opportunity to grow. So much of our anxiety and frustration is the result of feeling out of control and being overwhelmed by our circumstances instead of looking for the lessons that we may never have the opportunity to learn again. Maybe what you're dealing with now will equip you for another phase or stage of your life or give you the tools to help someone else. Don't waste a once-in-a-lifetime opportunity by focusing only on getting to the other side.

LEARN THE LESSONS THAT YOU CAN RIGHT NOW. YOU WILL NEVER LIVE THESE DAYS AGAIN.

Depending on what you are going through right now, the thought that you will never live these days again may be a really good one! But what you need to understand is that you also may never again have the opportunity to learn the lessons that these days present. We are so quick to try to end the pain of a difficult life without considering that success in the future may depend on the lessons learned today.

When I left the Marine Corps in 2003 I really believed that part of my life was behind me and that my time of service would never be anything more than a set of memories. I didn't grasp how significant that time in my life was and how it could be used to help others.

Nearly ten years later I was introduced to the Mighty Oaks Foundation and learned about the work that was being done to help men and women who have served in the military, with an emphasis on those who have served in combat. Since then, I have had the privilege of working with countless veterans and active duty military members, trying to help them understand that there is hope and purpose beyond their service and despite their personal or combat trauma.

What's crazy is that the very thing that qualifies me to have a part in this is the thing that I thought I was walking away from. I loved the Marine Corps and my time of service will forever be one of the things

I am most proud of. It was the only thing I wanted to do from the time I was young until the time I finally left. But what I failed to understand was that the lessons I learned and the experiences I had as a Marine were preparing me for another stage of life that I could not even comprehend while I was there. While my time in combat was much shorter than that of so many of the folks I now have the privilege of working with, it did provide the common ground that allows me to speak truth into their lives.

There were, of course, many personal lessons as well. Lessons that I should have appreciated more when I was learning them. For example:

- I watched the planning of an event the size of the Iraq invasion and then saw it all come together despite an incredibly chaotic environment. The lesson: if you have planned and rehearsed and done all that you can to prepare, you can come out on top even when things do not go exactly according to plan. Chaos does not need to dictate success or failure.

- I saw young men from every imaginable background, some less than a year out of high school, do things that most of the country would not even have the ability to comprehend, much less accomplish. The lesson: neither age, background, nor so many of the other standards we use to measure people ever tell the whole story. People will rise to the challenge when necessary.

- I saw oppressed people living lives of joy. We talked to farmers who had the means of production taken from them and city folks who had to deal with everyday situations unimaginable to most Americans. Although they wanted better lives for themselves and their families, they still made the best of their situations and lived incredibly resilient lives. The lesson: your circumstances do not dictate your joy unless you allow them to. It is possible to be happy even when your happiness does not make sense to those on the outside.

• I watched men of rank lead with the best interests of their subordinates in mind. The lesson: even in the chaos and confusion of combat, leaders who serve others are the leaders who win. The principle of servant leadership was modeled in a way that would impact my own understanding of leadership in environments far different than the military or combat.

And there were many others. Lessons that I have now learned in retrospect instead of learning them as they came. I kept a journal while I was in Iraq, but not one entry dealt with a lesson learned that I would be able to use in my life outside of the Marine Corps. I am thankful for what I have learned by looking back, but I wonder how much I missed that would be valuable now. As difficult as your circumstances may be, use this time to learn everything that you possibly can. You never know how those lessons will be used in the future.

FIND THE GOOD.

Human nature is not usually overwhelmingly positive. There

are positive people, but if we're honest, that's not most of us. Your life may be going well, but one unkind word or rough couple of hours can steal the joy from all that good. We gravitate toward the bad and spend so much time focused on it that we fail to enjoy the good. I have no idea what you may be dealing with right now or what you are going to be dealing with before you finish reading this book. But I do know there is something good in your life that deserves your focus no matter how bad your situation seems.

I often look fondly on my time of service because the bad things I focused on while serving have faded in my memory. The good things I couldn't see at the time are now what I think of when I think of the Marine Corps. The long days and nights, the sometimes less-than gourmet food, the discomfort and the danger have given way to thoughts of purpose and clarity, brotherhood and the pursuit of something noble.

There is a joke among those who have served that all you talk about while you're in is getting out and all you talk about when you get out is what you did while you were in. Somehow I don't think that's unique to veterans. Don't pretend that everything is okay all the time; just decide that you are going to focus on the good and deal with the rest when you must. That will make even the most difficult of situations valuable and will help you embrace the moment.

WHAT YOU LEARN TODAY MAY BE EXACTLY WHAT YOU NEED IN THE FUTURE.

A worthwhile exercise for anyone serious about moving forward even when life is overwhelming is the exercise of keeping a journal. I have done this at various times in my life, but I usually do so with the wrong focus in mind. I journal about events or feelings or simply to process a decision that needs to be made. While none of these is bad, journaling to record the lessons you've learned is much more helpful.

The hardships and difficulties you are experiencing today are only wasted if you do not learn everything they are intended to teach. I do not believe in being overly introspective, but we can redeem the moments we have if we are intentional about letting those moments shape future decisions and actions.

The fight we found ourselves in at the bridge over the Saddam Canal changed the way I look at so many things. There are quite a few lessons that I missed in Iraq, but that event taught me two very important life principles:

1. You are only done, or dead, if you stop moving.

2. You are not that special. Neither combat nor life cares who you are or where you came from. The victory goes to the persistent, not to the perfect.

These principles have allowed me to keep going when I find myself overwhelmed or under-equipped. I know that I'm not capable enough or smart enough for so many of the situations that I find myself in, but I also know that if I just keep going, I will come out on the other side.

I have found myself in difficult circumstances because of bad decisions I've made. But a bad decision is only fatal if you stop moving.

Hanging on to this lesson helped me keep moving even when I knew that the difficulties were a result of my own bad decisions.

Those two principles have followed me and helped to guide me through countless difficulties and obstacles. I, along with several of the Marines in my platoon, should have been killed on top of that bridge. For reasons I cannot explain, we were not. That potentially tragic situation has been turned into good for my family and me because of the lessons that it taught me.

What about you? What lessons do you need to learn from the seemingly overwhelming situation you find yourself in today? What do you need to learn so that you can avoid finding yourself here again? One of the most important steps you can take when life seems to be falling apart around you is to embrace the moment by learning the lessons you will inevitably need in the future.

CONCLUSION

I sometimes wonder how much of my life I have wasted by simply trying to get to the other side of whatever I was doing without stopping long enough to embrace the moment. How many lessons have I missed, how many opportunities with my wife and kids, how many of the simple joys have I lost because I wasn't looking for them? I wonder how much anxiety and frustration I've dealt with that was unnecessary, that I wouldn't have experienced had I focused on the things I could control rather than worrying about the things I couldn't.

Life is often difficult. That's just how it is. You can't live a life free from difficulty, but you can decide not to be overwhelmed by it.

Instead of allowing your circumstances to dictate how you feel and living your life to get beyond all that is hard, decide that you will embrace the moment, see the good, and learn all that you can. It may just be that this moment is exactly what you need to be ready for the next.

EMBRACE THE MOMENT.

- *Learn the lessons that you can right now. You will never live these days again.*
- *Find the good.*
- *Understand that what you learn today may be exactly what you need in the future.*

CHAPTER 8 - FIND OUT WHAT'S REALLY KILLING YOU

When I think of some of the places we traveled through while pressing toward Baghdad, I remember them much as you might remember a dream. I know that it happened, but the exact details are a little blurry. Sometimes I remember places and events this way because of the time that has transpired since they took place, but others I remember this way because even when they were happening it felt like a dream.

Much of our travel was at night, which meant that we were often very tired and had a difficult time processing all that was going on in the dark. One such night took place in a village, the name and location of which I have long forgotten. One thing I will not forget is how strange it felt to be there and how disoriented we all were as we worked to get set in.

For a reason that was never clear to me, this village was in just the right place for an infantry battalion (one like ours) to set up a security position intended to keep the enemy from getting behind the rest of our regiment. Our objective was to get into the village in the middle of the night and set in this massive security line before the sun came up. We would be there before the enemy had a chance to disrupt our efforts. Unlike many of the others we had moved through, this village was big enough to contain several small buildings in addition to homes and a recently abandoned school.

As we made our way in that night, we came under fire from the enemy we were supposed to be setting up a security position against! We never stopped moving but engaged what seemed like ghosts with weapons on the side of the road as we moved quickly to our pre-designated spots on the ground. It was so dark that all we could see through our night vision devices was some movement and the flashes of rifle and RPG fire. It was a lot more like a drive-by shooting than a firefight and none of the Marines, as I recall, were injured.

By the time we got set in, all of that stopped. Maybe we caught them off guard and they were just engaging us as they made their way out of the village, or maybe they just wanted to harass us but didn't want to get hurt. Either way, we were able to get to our destination and experience a relatively peaceful night.

As the sun came up the next morning and we tried to make sense of the night before, it was clear that the regular Iraqi Army had recently been here. From the equipment and weapons that were left behind, it appeared that these were the enemy troops who had engaged us the night before. There were several bodies on the ground and in the vehicles that had been disabled, and none of the people who lived there were still home.

Apparently, the dead bodies in the street and in blown-up or shot-up vehicles were the result of a fight between anti-Saddam fighters and the Iraqi army they were trying to keep out. With those troops gone, the people who lived in the village began to come back, and it wasn't long before we were not only trying to figure out what had happened while holding our security position, but dealing with civilians trying to get back to their homes.

And then we came under fire again. Only this time it was not a large, high-volume attack, but seemingly random, once-in-a-while mortar rounds falling around us. This type of harassing fire was not unusual and generally came from someone unhappy that we were in their neighborhood. It was the equivalent of shooting a gun up into the air and waiting for the bullets to land somewhere; it was a form of protest. Rarely did anyone get hurt.

We only started to take this seriously when a round fell right in the middle of the area where our supply vehicles had set up and even hit (not fatally) one of the Marines working there. That was when we realized something more than random potshots were being fired, and we needed to respond.

DON'T BE TOO QUICK TO IDENTIFY YOUR PROBLEM.

When we experience a situation that causes difficulty either for us or those around us, it's important that we find the thing (or person or organization) that is actually causing the problem. We are quick to evaluate how we feel or what we perceive is taking place and identify that as the problem. This can lead to one of two things: we either dismiss the problem as something insignificant that will go away on its own, or we misidentify the problem and damage relationships because we have decided that they are the problem and need to go.

It is possible that a situation may resolve itself given enough time, but it is also possible that not dealing with a problem, waiting for it to go away, will make it much worse. If we had dealt with the mortar problem when it first presented instead of assuming that it would resolve itself, a Marine may not have been injured. Thankfully little damage was done, but the situation was definitely more serious than we initially thought. Take the time to figure out what's really going on before you decide what you will or will not do.

When it became clear that the rounds being fired at us were strategic, the order came for us to find the person responsible. With so many civilians now in the area we weren't sure where to look, but we started with the information we had. We believed that there was someone in an elevated position who could look out over the area and direct his mortar fire to the location of his choosing. There was only one place in the village that afforded that kind of view. Near the center of the village, with the best view of any of the buildings, was the local school.

The school building was a square, three-story building that, from the roof, had a view of the entire area. While it's hard to believe that a school would be used to direct fire on those who lived there and those who came to protect them, this was not uncommon in our experience. It didn't take long for us to figure out that churches, schools, and hospitals were the most dangerous buildings in any area where we would find ourselves.

The wisdom of Iraqi soldiers was that Americans would not engage anyone in these buildings. While we were careful not to engage buildings with civilians unnecessarily, we were not afraid to deal with ones that housed only the enemy. It's funny to think that our perceived "American values" would be used against us, but I don't blame them for trying. Regardless, it was very common to find enemy soldiers in these places traditionally reserved for peaceful or humanitarian activities.

As we made our way to the school it was clear that classes had not taken place there for some time. Oddly, there was also what sounded like a huge dog barking from somewhere inside one of the classrooms. Carefully but with the intent to catch anyone who meant harm to us or others, we began to search each floor and each room in the building.

It was small and did not take long, and we quickly found a classroom on the third floor that clearly had been housing a soldier for a couple of days. There was a sleeping area and food trash as well as all the equipment needed to direct fire on the village below. We didn't know when the room was last occupied, but it was clearly not that long ago. In another room we found a large and very angry dog tied up, apparently being used as an alarm.

It was disappointing not to find the soldier, but at least we had the satisfaction of having run him off and the hope that no one else would be hurt. It was also good to confirm that the real source of the mortar fire was a bad guy and not a disgruntled resident of the village. Satisfied that we had done everything we could, we gathered the items with intelligence value and made our way back to our vehicles.

THE REAL PROBLEM MAY TRY TO DISGUISE ITSELF OR BLEND IN.

Before we started our search of the school, we set up a security perimeter around the building so that no one could get in while we were searching and so that no one running out could get away. Thankfully, the Marines on the perimeter were professionals who understood their job.

When those of us who had been inside the school made our way out, several of the Marines had a man tied up on the ground while others kept the growing crowd of people away. As we had made our way in, this man had made his way out and tried to blend in to the gathered residents. He was not wearing a uniform but clearly did not fit in. When he was singled out and confronted, he tried to run but couldn't get away.

When we finally got him back to our headquarters area and he was interrogated by our interrogator translator team, he confessed to being an Iraqi army forward observer who was calling in mortar fire on our position. His job was to do as much damage as he could to keep us occupied while the rest of the soldiers who were there the night before got away. It sounded like he had drawn the short straw when the discussion over who would stay behind took place, but this was the guy. We weren't able to capture the mortar team that had been shooting at us from outside of the village, but we effectively ended the threat to both ourselves and the folks who lived in the town by searching for and capturing this remaining soldier.

Iraq became a difficult area for U.S. troops shortly after the war began because the enemy was not conventional. During our first days in Iraq, we were fighting an enemy who represented a specific government and dressed as the military of that government. They had uniforms and wore rank and unit insignias and were easy to identify, which made engagement straightforward.

Shortly after the opening weeks of the war, though, that changed. The enemy was hard to identify because they dressed and acted like everyone else and may or may not have represented Saddam's government. Many of the soldiers we've been fighting in Iraq since 2003 represented ideals instead of a political system.

The soldier we captured identified himself as a member of the Iraqi army, but he didn't want anyone to know it. He did his best to blend in and disguise himself as something he wasn't. This has been a problem for the military as it continues to operate in non-conventional wartime scenarios, and it's a problem for anyone who has ever dealt with a trial in their life.

The real problems that we deal with in life are often not what they appear to be on the surface. What we see is often just a symptom of the real problem. If we aren't careful, we can miss the real issue while dealing with something only related to the real problem.

When we cleared the school, we believed that we had dealt with the problem; in reality the problem was disguised as something else. It was only careful observation and placing the facts in the proper context that allowed us to deal with the actual problem. Then we knew how to deal with the rest of the events in that village. We finally understood what we needed to, but only after looking past what we thought was the problem so that we could see the actual problem.

Misidentifying the situations or relationships that are causing you harm can hurt you more than the problem itself. We want so badly to resolve conflict or put an end to something that has caused us pain that we fail to address the real issue. How many relationships have ended, jobs have been eliminated, and major, life-altering decisions have been made simply because a problem was not clearly understood?

Be careful that you aren't looking past the very thing you should be dealing with. It may take a little more time and effort, but both are a worthwhile investment if you want to win your battles.

YOU MIGHT NEED TO GET SOME HELP IDENTIFYING THE PROBLEM.

This scenario would have played out differently were it not for the team involved in making it happen. There were commanders who decided we needed to find the source of the problem, Marines inside the building, Marines outside the building, and Marines back at our command post who were able to interrogate our prisoner and find out what was going on. None of this would have happened if one Marine had set out on his own to figure it out. Most victories take place because a team is involved.

The same is true when we are dealing with difficult situations in our lives. Often when dealing with something difficult, we pull away from those who care about us and want to help us, deciding that we'll just do it on our own.

The problem with doing it on our own is that we are only able to see a problem from one perspective. We see things from where we're standing instead of getting a full view from somewhere else. This is why so much of the time we view our situation emotionally and respond in a way we later regret.

Also, if we don't allow others to help us, we don't have the ability to see what the real source of the problem is us. Truthfully, we are the ones who need to change more than we need other people or situations to change, but if we are unwilling to let others help us, then we will never be able to deal with the real problem.

Having people in your life who care about you and are willing to tell you the sometimes-difficult truth is essential if you are going to deal with the right problem instead of just dealing with what you feel is the right problem. Don't let pride or fear keep you from reaching out. Find those who care about your success and let them speak into your situation and then trust them enough to listen. If you try to do it on your own, the real problem may blend into the crowd and slip away.

CONCLUSION

It's impossible to move forward if we are unable or unwilling to deal with the issues causing problems in our lives. So often, though, even when we want to deal with those problems, we misidentify them and end up dealing with something that is not the problem at all.

I've talked before about how difficult counseling others can be. As someone who has spent most of my life working with people in a ministry setting, I have invested thousands of hours in trying to help men, women, and couples understand the source of whatever difficult situation they are involved in. I have counseled those struggling with relationship issues, personal tragedies and life transitions as well as all the other stuff that doesn't really fall into a particular category.

While I am thankful for the opportunity to help those who are going through a hard time, it is extremely difficult to help those who are struggling to see their struggles as they actually are. I have the same problem personally, by the way, which I am sure is a challenge to those who have counseled me along the way.

What makes this difficult most of the time is that we want the problem to be something other than it is. We want it to be something that we can cut out or that will resolve itself over time. So much of a counselor's job is helping the one who is being counseled to understand their struggles in their appropriate context.

I have counseled those who have lost a loved one and decide, in the middle of that pain, that a major life change is in order. They misidentify the cause of their pain as their job or a relationship instead of a painful personal loss and make decisions they later regret. I've counseled couples who eventually quit on their marriage because they perceive an attitude or stage of life to be the problem when really it's a brokenness that could be healed if only they were willing to work. I have counseled veterans who tie all of their struggles to a moment in combat when they are really the result of a series of bad decisions that can be addressed and worked through. This is what makes counseling so difficult. Problems cannot be resolved until they are first properly, and clearly, identified.

What's really killing you? One of the reasons we often stay where we are and die instead of getting up and marching forward is because we think we are dealing with one thing when really we should be dealing with something else! Don't allow emotions, fatigue, fear, or the words of those who mean you harm to keep you from seeing your situation, good or bad, as it is. As hard as it may be when you are hurting, take the time to step back, get perspective, and hear from those who want what is best for you so you can grow through these often-difficult times. Learn to clearly define what is killing you so that you can take the steps to eliminate it and move on. On the other side of the battle, you will be glad that you did.

FIND OUT WHAT'S REALLY KILLING YOU.

- *Don't be too quick to identify your problem.*
- *The real problem may try to disguise itself or blend in.*
- *You might need to get some help identifying the problem.*

CHAPTER 9 - DECIDE: YOU WON'T GIVE UP

Forty years is a long time. I have a hard time being patient if a car ride takes forty minutes. Imagine being told by God that you would spend the next forty years wandering around in the desert because of a decision you had no part in!

This is exactly the conversation that God had with Moses after the Israelites refused to go into the land He had promised to them. Because of their rebellion, He said, they would spend the next forty years living in the desert and would only be able to go into the Promised Land once every adult who had been a part of the rebellion died.

Of the twelve spies who went in to look at the land, only two made it through this time of desert wandering: Joshua and Caleb. I often wonder what Caleb thought as he heard Moses explain what was going to happen. What was his first thought when he realized that the next forty years of his life would basically, at least from his perspective, be a waste? He would experience punishment because of the decisions of others, and there was nothing he could do about it.

As crazy as the story of the Exodus and the children of Israel is, it captures how so much of life works. It's true that we often end up in difficult situations because of our own bad decisions, but there are also quite a few difficult situations we find ourselves in because of the bad decisions of others.

When I bring a trial into my life because of something I did, I feel the need to talk about grace and forgiveness. Even when my bad decisions bring difficulty or pain into the lives of others, I expect them to deal with it and continue to love me. When the pain in my life is the consequence of someone else's bad decisions, though, I have a hard time remembering what grace even means. Instead of loving and forgiving, I want them to pay. I certainly don't want to walk around in the desert for the next forty years because of what they did. It feels unjust to suffer because of another person's mistake, and if we aren't careful, it can cause us to question the very goodness of God. We did not choose this fight.

If you are reading the story of Caleb for the first time, you may conclude that he would not stay with a nation being punished by God. He had every reason to pack up his family and find his own place to live, and I don't think anyone would have questioned his decision to do so. God said that he and Joshua were the only two spies who would not die in the wilderness which, if I was Caleb, would have been a green light to leave.

But that's not what he did. One of the most fascinating aspects of this part of the story to me is the silence of Caleb once God's judgment was given. We know that he was a leader of his tribe and can assume that people knew he was a leader because he made good decisions and was not afraid to show others what they needed to do. When he came back from viewing the land, he told the nation how amazing it was and then pleaded with them to trust God. He was not afraid to speak up, and if he was like most other leaders that I've known, he probably already had an alternate plan to wandering in the desert. But he said nothing and did nothing. Nothing, at least, other than decide to trust God and hang on until this "storm" was over.

And here we learn a very important lesson: When you find yourself in the desert and feel like you are out of control and out of options, you have two choices: You can die like everyone else or you can decide to push through. It may sound like a simple thing, but that simple decision will be the difference between making it to the promised land that God has already prepared for you, or not.

We don't have recorded anywhere that Caleb had a family meeting to decide what he was going to do. But somewhere along the way he decided to simply trust God. He decided, before he needed to, that regardless of what may come in his life, he was not going to quit. Far too many people wait to decide what they are going to do until they determine how difficult it's going to be. That may work in some places, but if you wait to decide if you are going to quit until you find out how hard something is, you might as well quit now because you are not going to make it. A key element of long marriages, strong relationships, successful careers, and living lives of value is that pre-decision to simply keep going.

Another great example of this principle at work is found in the life of Jesus. While we all like to ask the question, "Why do bad things happen to good people," we tend to forget that there has only ever been one good person. As good as we like to think we are, most honest people will admit that they aren't that good. Most of us want to be good and try to be good but understand the truth of Romans 3:23 that "all have sinned."

Jesus, however, is perfect. I Peter 1:19 calls Jesus a "lamb without blemish and without spot." He is perfect, which qualified Him to stand in our place and pay for our sin on the cross. Someone has to pay for our sin, and God loves us so much that he provided Jesus to do just that (John 3:16). What's crazy about this is that Jesus did not deserve to die on the cross—we did! He experienced the anguish of being crucified because of what someone else (humanity) had done. But he did it willingly and offers the gift of salvation that was purchased freely to all who will receive. He is God, and we are not.

The words of Hebrews 12 teach us so much. Verses 2-3 of this chapter say this: "Looking unto Jesus the author and finisher of our faith; who for the joy that was set before him endured the cross, despising the shame, and is set down at the right hand of the throne of God. For consider him that endured such contradiction of sinners against himself, lest ye be wearied and faint in your minds." These verses tell us that when the trials we are enduring begin to overwhelm us, we need to continue moving forward toward the prize that caused us to start in the first place. That's what Jesus did, and that's what we should do as well.

When you find yourself in the desert, and we all will, even when it's not our fault, push through. It's the only way you will ever get to the other side.

Section 4:

CHANGE IS INEVITABLE - DON'T BE SURPRISED WHEN IT HAPPENS

CHAPTER 10 - JUST KEEP MOVING

From the moment we started talking about going into Iraq everyone knew that the ultimate destination was the capital city of Baghdad. Every plan ended with us in Baghdad, every battle study was the study of a time another country pushed troops toward Baghdad, and the guy we were trying to get rid of lived there. It all just made sense. Funny how these things happen.

So when the time to go into Baghdad finally arrived, it just seemed like the next natural step on this journey that we had been taking. It would be, however, the most difficult day I had experienced up to that point in my life.

Baghdad is a city of several million people and has long been one of the most modern cities in the Middle East, attracting visitors from all over the world. When I am trying to provide some context for those who haven't been there, I always explain that being in Baghdad is a little bit like being in Los Angeles. It is a massive city with a massive population, an airport, university, and anything any other modern city would have. Very different than the farms and small villages that we had grown accustomed to seeing in the southern part of the country. In 2003, it was of strategic importance because it was the seat of life in Iraq and because it held the homes of Saddam Hussein and his sons.

The plan for securing the city was to approach from both the south and the north east, which sounds simple but was an event that included thousands of troops and coordination from the top commanders in the United States. The army would push in on April 9 from the south, and the Marine Corps would then move in the early hours of April 10 from the North East.

All seemed to be going well. The Army's Third Infantry Division met little resistance securing strategic objectives and toppling the large statue of the now deposed dictator Saddam Hussein that graced the center of the city.

While that was taking place, Fifth Marines was sitting on the outskirts of the city in a small suburb. My platoon was at a checkpoint controlling civilian traffic. Sometime in the middle of the day on the 9th the decision was made that our battalion would be the battalion from Fifth Marines that would lead the move into the city and then make our way to the presidential palace that sat on the banks of the Tigris river.

Coordination began for a move that would start just after midnight. I don't always do everything right, but I have found that if I show up on time to my appointed place of duty, I generally do pretty well. Since I pride myself on being where I'm supposed to be when I'm supposed to be there, you'd think that, given the magnitude of the event in front of us, I would have not been late when the instructions were given out. But because my platoon was spread out at the checkpoint, I was so late getting to the briefing area that the plan for the movement had already been given.

I was told what we would need to do once the battalion made it to the Presidential Palace and also told not to worry about getting there because we would follow one of the large amphibious tractors (Amtrack) that would be carrying Marines. The movement to the palace was not expected to be a difficult one, so I wasn't too concerned about not knowing the route.

As we began just after midnight, it was clear that this was not going to be a simple movement into a quiet city. We had only gone a short distance when a truck parked on the road exploded. This truck was just a few vehicles in front of me, and it took me a minute to figure out what was going on.

Your mind plays tricks on you in moments like these, and for some reason I thought that one of our gunners had caused the truck, parked quietly on the road, to explode. The explosion happened as the first vehicles in our battalion column came alongside, most likely as a signal to the enemy soldiers who were waiting for us.

No one was hurt in that explosion, but once that vehicle exploded, there was no more silence until late into the next night. What we hoped would be a quiet, uneventful trip was an ambush by an enemy who was clearly making what they thought was a last stand. They fired Rocket Propelled Grenades (RPG) and AK 47's from the street and the buildings that lined the street and inflicted tremendous damage to our vehicles. They were doing their best to keep us from getting to our objective.

It must have been a little bit like the shooting gallery at a fair for them since our entire battalion, nearly twelve hundred marines in various vehicles, was moving as a column on the road. It was impossible for us to get cover while being fired down upon from elevated positions. As they fired, doors and windows were torn off of Humvee's, tires were flattened, and packs hanging on the side of Amphibious Tractors were destroyed.

More than seventy marines suffered injury during that firefight, but miraculously, we had only one KIA. The Marine who was killed in action was Gunnery Sergeant Jeffrey Bohr, an amazing human being with a long life of military service, who received a silver star for his actions during the firefight that would take his life. As difficult as it was for the battalion to lose Gunny Bohr, it is incredible, and unexplainable, how we did not lose many more that day.

As we made our way through the city streets, our long column of vehicles got turned around, with half heading one direction and the other heading another. We were driving down a two-way street with a barrier between lanes, only feet away from each other while traveling two different directions. Because we were being engaged from buildings on both sides of the road, this meant that each column of our vehicles was firing over the adjacent column to deal with the shooters in the windows. The chaos was incredible as enemy tracer rounds and RPG's came at us while our own tracer rounds were going both directions over our heads. Add to this the darkness, radio communication, a city where none of us had ever been, and vehicles and Marines being hit, and it is incredible we were able to keep going.

This was not what we (at least not me) expected, but after planning, you deal with what is in front of you. Some people get so hung up when things don't go according to their plan that they are never able to make any forward progress or, at best, make very slow progress. The reality is that you can only do what you can do. Plan and prepare, but as we've said already, expect the situation to change, and when it does, deal with it. The reason that we plan and prepare is to eliminate as many variables as possible so that when the situation does change, we will be able to keep moving.

WHEN YOU DON'T KNOW WHICH WAY TO GO, PICK ONE AND KEEP MOVING.

As the early morning light began to break, our situation began to improve. Now we could at least see far enough down the roads we were traveling to make educated decisions about routes. And then things changed again.

The vehicle my platoon was following, the one leading us because I missed the brief, turned into an alley with all of us behind it. The driver of that vehicle jumped out and as quickly as he could made his way to me to say that he didn't know exactly where we were or how to get to where we needed to go. He had been relying on his onboard GPS system to help him navigate, but because of damage to his vehicle, the system stopped working. This was a problem because I had only been told what to do once we got to our objective, but I didn't know where that was. I didn't even know there was a second Presidential Palace in Baghdad until I found out we were going there!

I called our battalion commander on the radio and, in the middle of everything else that he was dealing with, asked if he could give me the coordinate. This felt a bit like having your kid ask you from the backseat, "Are we there yet?" while you drive lost through downtown Los Angeles (only with a whole lot of people trying to kill you). All he could tell me was to go south, which I assumed meant turn left, and then figure it out. (Looking back, I wonder how he knew to give me that direction since he didn't know where I was.)

Not knowing how I was going to figure it out but also not wanting anyone to know that, I told the column of vehicles to follow me as I had my vehicle pull out of the alley and turn left onto the main road. I have never been good with directions and even now sometimes need to use the GPS to get to my house, but I didn't know what else to do. I figured that once we got onto the main road there would be something that would help me know what to do next. I realize that it sounds a little crazy given all that was going on and the horrible odds I had of getting us out of there, but as we turned left, the company of vehicles that I was supposed to link up with pulled onto the street in front of us. For anyone watching it would have looked like a perfectly coordinated link-up, but in reality it was just one of the many unexplainable events of that day.

IT DOESN'T ALL HAVE TO MAKE SENSE. JUST DO WHAT YOU KNOW IS RIGHT AND DON'T WORRY ABOUT THE REST.

When we finally arrived at the Presidential Palace my job was to set my eighteen vehicles in a screen line in front of the palace so that the rest of the battalion could come in behind us and secure the actual facility. Again, the chances of that working were not very good, but in execution it looked like we had rehearsed and set in perfectly. When the rest of the battalion finally made it inside, we also made our way to the inside of the palace compound and removed our vehicle-mounted weapons from the vehicles, placing them where they could be used to defend against the enemy in the street.

The environment continued to be absolutely chaotic. No one who fought against us that day was a regular Iraqi Army soldier and no one wore a uniform, which made it extremely difficult to know who was good and who was bad. In a city that size, there were a lot of people just trying to get out. But there were also a lot of people who were trying to do harm. We did our best to discern between the two, but the confusion of the moment along with the need to defend our position made that very difficult.

As I stood on a rooftop next to one of our machine gun positions I watched men in civilian clothes shoot rifles and RPG's, while another group of men used an ambulance to get as close to us as they could and then jumped out of the back and started engaging. As the battle went on, many of these fighters began to take refuge in a Mosque a few blocks from our position. As mentioned earlier, our enemy would use American ideals, things such as the sanctity of life and the importance of places of worship, to keep us from dealing with them. Once we figured out what they were doing, though, we did what was necessary to win.

There are times in life when the events around you will make absolutely no sense. You will try to figure it out, and eventually you might, but in the moment, it will be hard to know what to do next. As the hours of the battle in Baghdad began to stack up, the one thing that got us through was that even in the confusion, we just kept doing the next thing.

That wasn't necessarily easy. Years of training combined with focused leadership equipped us to do the next thing well, but when we could not see the big picture, we dealt with what was in front of us. There were some high-level decisions being made and intelligence being processed, but our job at that moment was to do our job and let others do theirs.

When the world feels like it's spinning out of control, it's possible to become so overwhelmed with all that's going on that you freeze up, unable to do anything. Just do what you know to do and do it well. Take the step in front of you and worry about the one after that when you get there.

THE MORNING WILL COME.

As the day wore on, we were able to get some amazing support from both the Air National Guard and Marine Air. While Marine air was re-supplying and doing medevac off the back lawn of the palace, A-10 Warthogs were providing close air support for those fighting in the front. Of the many sights and sounds in Baghdad that day, one sound I will never forget is the sound of the A-10 firing down on the enemy in front of our position. Somehow hearing that sound helps you to know that everything is going to be okay.

By the time it got dark again, most of the fighting had stopped. Intelligence sources told us that there would be a counter-attack later that night, but after a well-placed air-dropped munition a few hours later, the fighting was over. After a day like that, we weren't sure what the night would be like, but we were able to rotate through a watch and rest schedule that got everyone back on track. The combination of physical and emotional exhaustion made any opportunity to rest a welcome reprieve.

The next morning, as the sun started to come up, I walked to each of our machine gun positions spread out across the front side of the palace grounds. Some were at gates and some were on roofs, but all were in a position to protect us should a counter-attack come. I wanted to make sure that everyone was okay and that we were ready for whatever would happen next. As I made my way from one position to the next I was struck with just how peaceful it was. The air was still and cool and extremely quiet. How amazing that the same place twenty-four hours earlier could not have been more out of control. I didn't spend enough time in Iraq appreciating what was happening around me, but that morning I could not miss the contrast of one day and the next.

I think we forget sometimes that the quiet morning will eventually come. As bad as a situation may seem right now, if we are patient and hold on to the hope that we've been given, we will come out on the other side. As the battles rage in the darkness of night and fatigue begins to overwhelm us, we start to believe that life will always be this way. We know that situations like this can't last forever, but the enemy is so powerful and the way forward so confusing that we don't know how it will ever end. But it will. The morning always comes, and the battles always end. Our job is to simply hang on to hope and take the next step.

Don't give up. You're going to make it.

CONCLUSION

There were a lot of memorable events during our time in Iraq, but none quite as memorable as our push into Baghdad. It was a day of intense combat, sometimes overwhelming confusion, loss, and a fight for survival contrasted with an incredible fighting spirit, Marines who did exactly what was necessary to win, and the defeat of an enemy who had every advantage. An entire book could be written dealing with life lessons from that one twenty-four-hour period, but for me, one of the major lessons learned was that there are times when all you can do is keep moving. Don't allow a change of plans or the fog of war to keep you from taking the next step. Those who win life's battles are not those who have it all figured out when they start. Winners understand that the key to victory is doing your best while taking the next step forward.

JUST KEEP MOVING.

- *When you don't know which way to go, pick one and keep moving.*
- *It doesn't all have to make sense. Just do what you know is right and don't worry about the rest.*
- *The morning will come.*

CHAPTER 11 - THE ENEMY IS NOT AS GOOD AS YOU THINK

The movement across the berm separating northern Kuwait and Southern Iraq was a move into the unknown. We had quite a bit of intelligence about the Iraqi military, but their actual capability and willingness to fight was largely unknown. The experience of Desert Storm in the early 90's caused some to believe that we would have very little resistance, but pushing an army out of a neighboring country is very different than trying to kick them out of their own.

We were told before the invasion that occupation had never been done well in Iraq. Well-equipped and determined enemies had lost here, and we were concerned that it could happen again. Based on the rhetoric of Saddam Hussein and his military underlings along with the belief that he had and would use chemical weapons, predictions regarding the number of U.S. casualties were not good. At the very least we believed that we would face the well-publicized Republican Guard, who, at least in their billing, were an elite military force forged in the battles of the Iran and Iraq conflict in the 80's. Chemical weapons, an elite military force and rumors of modern weapons and tanks projected an image of the enemy that was hard to believe.

Even though it was hard to believe, this was the enemy we prepared for. We discussed and war-gamed every possible scenario that we might face and then did our best to be ready. And very little went according to plan. In fact, the United States and its allies spent almost fifteen years trying to figure this enemy out and adjusting as they learned. Over this period nearly everything related to fighting in Iraq changed. The weapons and equipment changed to more effectively deal with an unconventional force. Tactics changed to deal with an enemy representing an ideology instead of a country. Politics changed in an ongoing attempt to build a stable government. The only thing consistent in this war on terror was the constant need to adjust to change. It was the only way that any progress was made.

One of the major changes we needed to make when moving into Iraq was a change in the way we viewed the enemy. We needed to take them seriously, of course, but could not afford to let them gain the mental upper hand by believing that they were better prepared or better equipped for this fight than we were. Every day we learned something new about them and every day we had to adjust to this new information.

If we aren't willing or able to adjust to an enemy that is consistently changing, we will have a hard time coming out on top. We need to expect the enemy to change and then be ready to change based on new information and understanding. We must fight against a mindset that keeps us stuck in what we were told or falsely believed. The enemy is there to win, and we must do everything we can to keep that from happening.

THE ENEMY WANTS YOU TO THINK THEY'RE BETTER THAN THEY ACTUALLY ARE.

This became clear when we engaged the Iraqi army on the first night of the war. To be sure, there were some intense moments of fighting, but the army was not nearly as capable or well-armed as we were led to believe, and most had very little will to fight. Very quickly the composition of the enemy changed from a conventional to a very unconventional force.

The propaganda about the uniformed military was much better than the soldiers themselves. During the first few days of the war, we had hundreds of uniformed soldiers surrender to us without a fight. Many of them were hungry and scared and just wanted to go back to their homes. As we cleared buildings we found uniforms discarded by soldiers who had no desire to lose their lives in "Saddam's war." There were still those who wanted to fight and cause us harm, but that wasn't most of them. Most people were as happy to see their dictator toppled as we were to make it happen.

This has been true in every battle or fight, physical or otherwise, I have ever been involved in. As bad as some things can be, they are rarely as bad as we make them out to be in our minds. It turns out that each of us has a pretty good propaganda machine inside of us that builds and projects an image of the enemies in our lives that just isn't true. But we believe it because we have imagined it.

I'm not suggesting that we underestimate our enemy. We just need to make sure we are fighting an enemy who actually exists. Sometimes the only power that your enemy has is what you think about him. Our perception of the enemy can be a powerful weapon against us and keeps many of us from moving forward when life doesn't go as we thought it would. We begin to imagine every possible bad outcome of fighting the enemy in front of us and defeat ourselves because of what we believe could happen.

We can win, but only if we fight the enemy that exists. This may take some adjustment in our mindset or a change to our plan, but we will lose otherwise.

YOU MAY NOT KNOW WHAT'S WAITING FOR YOU, BUT YOU WILL NOT WIN UNTIL YOU CROSS THE LINE.

Even though the enemy was uncertain and the potential for loss was high, when the decision to cross the berm into Iraq was made we went forward and trusted that we were prepared for whatever was on the other side.

That night was one that I will never forget. We had planned and prepared and practiced, but while it was happening it felt like a dream. The night was pitch black except for the artillery rounds screaming through the sky to prep the battlefield minutes before we would get there. The occasional explosion would light up the night, but other than that, it was dark.

But just as we had rehearsed, we followed our lanes of travel and moved from the safety of Kuwait into the much debated, much anticipated unknown of Iraq. And in the dark, smoke-filled night, we experienced something we had never experienced in training. Watching the bright tracer rounds designed to keep us on target at night fired out of our weapons traveling down range was not unusual. Watching enemy tracer rounds come back our direction was. In sheer volume we were firing many more rounds on our objective than the Iraqi soldiers, but knowing that someone out in the dark was firing back took a few minutes to fully comprehend.

By the time the sun came up First Battalion Fifth Marines was sitting on the first objective of the war and beginning, among other things, to process the Iraqi soldiers who decided they did not want to fight. The opening hours of the war in Iraq, with friendly casualty projections in the thousands, had come and gone with very few American troops injured. Later that morning we would lose the first KIA of the war, Lt. Shane Childers, but the regular army soldiers who were responsible for repelling our first attack demonstrated that, for the most part, the enemy was all hype and little substance.

From a strategic, military standpoint, our overwhelming success the first few days of the war can be explained. Overwhelming force coupled with incredible planning and strong leadership paved the way for a decisive victory. But even with all those pieces working together, the way was made easier by an enemy who was ill-prepared and lacked the will to fight and die.

But here's the thing: we would not have known that if the decision makers had bought into the hype and kept us from doing what we were there to do. The potential for disaster has kept more than one military commander in history from leading men into battle, and our leaders faced the same dilemma. They had to decide that the only way to find out the true capability of the enemy was to engage them because the cost of doing nothing was much higher than any potential loss that would come from moving forward.

And that's how it works. You will never know how big the battle or how strong the enemy unless you are willing to cross the berm and go forward. You need to come to a place in your own heart and mind where you believe the loss of doing nothing is greater than the potential loss of taking whatever the next step is. Your enemy begins to lose strength and power the minute you begin to engage him, but some will never even take that step because they believe what they have heard or imagined, with no way of knowing whether it's true.

THE UNEXPECTED IS THE REAL ENEMY.

Engaging the enemy was never the hardest part about being in Iraq during those early days of the war. The only enemy we prepared for was the kind that wore uniforms and wanted to hurt us. The real enemy came in the form of sleep deprivation, broken vehicles, keeping the supply vehicles close enough to get what we needed, and a giant sandstorm. We also had moments when Marines got sick of being in a confined space together for hours on end and the long hours of boredom. There were enemies who worked to keep us from accomplishing our mission, but the ones that did us the most harm were not the ones we planned for.

This is one of the big dangers that comes when we focus on how we believe the enemy will hurt us and imagine all the ways we can be defeated. When we focus on an imaginary enemy, we take our eyes off the things that can actually do us damage. We need to plan based on the best information we have, but we can't overlook the other areas that we need to tend to. Be willing to shift your focus from what you thought you'd have to deal with to the unexpected enemies who can cause real harm.

CONCLUSION

We will always have people and circumstances that make it difficult for us to do what we believe we should do. When those enemies come, how should we respond? Some will build the enemy up so big in their minds that all they can do is nothing. They allow him to beat them before the first engagement.

Your enemy, whether a person or a circumstance, is always going to seem bigger than he really is until you are willing to deal with him to the best of your ability. The situation may have changed, and the enemy may be different than you expected. See him as he really is and do what you must to win.

THE ENEMY IS NOT AS GOOD AS YOU THINK.

- *The enemy wants you to think they are worse than they are.*
- *You may not know what's waiting for you, but you will not win until you cross the line.*
- *The unexpected is the real enemy.*

CHAPTER 12 - WINNING IS ABOUT RELATIONSHIPS

Much has been written on the importance of a team for success in life and business. Military schools emphasize the strength that comes from the unit and the potential for failure that exists when the unit falls apart. As I trained to be a Marine infantry leader for over a year, I was taught how to lead a team and my platoon as a part of a larger team. Everyone understood their place as well as the need to work together toward a common mission.

What I learned during combat operations in Iraq, though, is that simply having a team is not enough. Having the right team is essential to any victory, but winning is about more than just having the right people in the right place. It is about the relationships among team members that go beyond a skill set or proficiency. It is a relationship built over time that allows you to look into the eyes of those on your team and know what they're thinking. It's about understanding when to push and when to pull back because you know how heavy the load can become before the team will begin to fall apart. Winning is not simply about the team; it's about relationships.

I could have put this chapter in a few different places in this book, but I included it in this section because it's nearly impossible to adjust quickly and efficiently to change without the relationships that hold a team together. A team can win when everything goes according to plan. And when the plan needs to change because the situation has changed, you need more than a team. You need a group of people who understand each other and care for each other and are willing to adjust even though it may be difficult. You need relationships.

YOU CAN'T WIN ALONE.

It's impossible to win alone, whether in life or in combat. But many try. We go through life and complain about the trials and the battles and how much we have to carry when in reality, we were never designed to fight these battles alone.

We live in a society that loves superheroes and the idea that one person with a special power or an inhuman drive can save the world alone. But that's not how real life works. And even though we know that real life is not like what we see on the big screen, we let shame or guilt or pride keep us from letting others help us move forward into the life we were created to live.

When I think about the success we had in Iraq, I cannot think about it without thinking of the thousands of people involved in bringing it all together, from those at the highest levels of leadership to the seventeen- and eighteen-year-old service members who had finished high school only months earlier. Success in combat is the result of thousands of pieces all coming together at the right place and the right time. It's about the relationships between different branches of service (and countries of service, in many cases), different experiences and backgrounds built on a common goal with common objectives.

Relationships that bring different people together for a unified purpose are the key to overcoming incredible difficulty and finding success.

YOU DON'T JUST NEED PEOPLE; YOU NEED THE RIGHT PEOPLE.

Looking back at the team I had the privilege of being a part of while serving in Iraq both humbles and awes me. The chain of command went way above me, but our division commander was the current Secretary of Defense James Mattis and our regimental commander was the current Chairman of the Joint Chiefs of Staff General Joe Dunford! It is incredible to me to even think about that. Our battalion leadership were men of equally incredible character and skill as military leaders and unbelievable mentors. I had then, and still have today, a respect for each one of these men that I've had for very few others.

And then my own team. I had the privilege of leading the Counter-Mechanized Platoon for two years, which included our time in Iraq. The largest platoon in the battalion (we had 72 Marines and went up to 84 with attachments in Iraq), we were largely independent, which gave us the opportunity to train closely and get to know each other in a way that made communication with very few words possible. This closeness of relationship taught us to understand the strengths and weaknesses of the team and adjust where necessary.

This all came together as we navigated the many friction points we experienced as we made our way from Kuwait to Baghdad. We were able to take care of our vehicles and weapons systems all while operating in an extremely difficult environment, successfully completing each mission, and bringing everyone home when it was all over. I have often said that my time in Iraq is one of the greatest sources of pride in my life, and what made it so were the men with whom I had the honor of serving. I would do it all over again as long as I could do it with the same team.

Success is not just about having a team; it is about having the right team. It is about having relationships at every level that make the team better.

You'll know you have the right relationships in your life when your relationships are with those who have stayed when your chances of survival were not very good. Those are the relationships you need to invest in.

This is true in combat, and this is true in life. Those who stay when everyone else leaves are the ones who care about *you* more than they care about your success or failure. Who runs with you toward the enemy? Hang on to them. They will still be there when the dust settles. That is your team. That team is built on real relationships.

RELATIONSHIPS ARE TWO-WAY. YOU NEED THE PEOPLE WHO ALSO NEED YOU.

I did not understand this when I was a part of this incredible Marine Corps team, but relationships go two ways. This is the difference between simply using someone to get what you want and having a relationship that is mutually beneficial. In the years since I left the Marine Corps I have had the opportunity to connect with many of the men with whom I served and, hopefully, add the same value to their lives that they have to mine. I have learned that the relationships you need in your life are not relationships that end when an event or crisis ends. The relationship may look different as time goes on, but it doesn't end because we never stop needing each other.

A team may dissolve. Relationships last.

CONCLUSION

We were never meant to live alone, and we are not meant to fight alone. Our success in this life is largely determined by the team we have around us. That team, though, is only as good as the relationships that hold it together.

I have a friend who says it this way: "Show me your friends, and I will show you your future." What a great statement. The people whom you trust and the people who care for you are the people who will help you see obstacles, deal with the enemies that present themselves, experience victory when victory seems out of reach, and adjust to a world that is forever changing. Get the right team with the right people, held together by authentic relationships, and you will be unstoppable.

WINNING IS ABOUT RELATIONSHIPS.

- *You can't win alone.*
- *You don't just need people; you need the right people.*
- *Relationships are two-way. You need the people who also need you.*

CHAPTER 13 - DECIDE: YOU WILL ADJUST WITH THE CIRCUMSTANCES

The time in the desert was finally coming to an end, and it was time for the Israelites to enter the land that God had prepared for them. Instead of crossing the Red Sea, they would cross the Jordan River, but they were finally ready to do what God had directed forty years earlier. As they prepared for this next step in their journey, something very interesting happened. Before they crossed the Jordan River and made their way to the first city in the Promised Land, Joshua, the new leader of Israel, had twelve men, one from each tribe, go into the land as spies and come back with a report to the rest of the nation.

Once again, I wonder what Caleb was thinking while all of this was taking place. I wonder if he thought that these spies might mess it up like the last ones did and he would be stuck marching through the desert again. I wonder if he considered the irony of this decision since it was this very thing a generation earlier that brought God's judgment on them.

We don't know what he was thinking, but the image here is really important. Just because a previous generation of Israelites had rebelled against God's plan does not mean that God was walking away from what He said He was going to do. I think that by having a whole new set of spies go into the land and come back with a report for the nation, God was saying, "I am still in control, I still have a plan, and I am going to set everything right."

Perhaps Caleb was encouraged by what he saw with this new set of spies. I'm sure that he had lost friends and family members, not to mention a significant period of his life, because a group of people decided to go their own way, and yet now he was finally seeing God do what He said He would do.

The occupation of the land, however, would not happen without a significant amount of work. They were finally, after forty long years, back to the place they were supposed to be, but now they would have to fight!

Imagine what must have been going on in his heart and head. Forty years earlier when he was forty years of age he attempted to do right but ended up marching through the desert. Now, at age eighty, he was back to where he started but would have to fight to get what God had promised. Beginning an occupation campaign when you are forty is one thing. Starting it at eighty is something entirely different. But again, just as he had in the past, he made the necessary adjustments and pressed on.

We do not need to change our character or convictions because those around us change. Caleb didn't change either of those when it would have been very easy to do so. But when the battle changes, when the circumstances of the fight change or shift, we need to be willing to make the necessary adjustments to fight and win.

When the fight changes, many are unwilling to change so that they can win the fight. Nothing ever goes according to plan, and if we expect it to, we will lose. Excuses given for being unwilling to change are things like, "I tried this before and it didn't work," or, "I have never done this before and got by just fine," or maybe, "I could have done this when I was younger, but my time has passed."

Caleb could have made any of these excuses and been justified in doing so. But he didn't. When the situation changed and it was time to fight, eighty-year-old Caleb laced up his boots (or sandals), sharpened his sword, and moved to the front of the fight-the-bad-guys line (I may have made up that last one). The point is this. Caleb never changed who he was, but he adjusted what he did to fight and win the battle in front of him.

If you are going to win, if you are going to march when it would be easier to just stay where you are and die, you need to expect things to change and then make the necessary adjustments to come out on top. Trust God. Know that He will do what He said He would do. Be ready to fight. March forward.

Section 5:

WHEN YOU ARE STUCK, YOU ONLY HAVE TWO OPTIONS: MARCH OR DIE

CHAPTER 14 - DON'T STOP FIGHTING

Don't Stop Fighting | 145

It's amazing how quickly circumstances can change. April 10 in Baghdad was the most intense fighting of our time in Iraq and became an event that was written about and analyzed for several years afterward. The intensity of the battle and the number of American troops involved was something that we had not seen in even the largest training exercises.

As I walked the palace grounds to check on Marines early on the morning of April 11, I talked with Lt. Colonel Padilla who was doing the same. We talked for just a minute before moving on, and he encouraged me to make sure that the Marines in my platoon were ready for another difficult day of fighting.

But the fighting never came. We went from fighting our way into a city against a well-armed force that didn't want us there to walking the streets where men, women, and children thanked us for coming in the best way they knew how. After getting into the city we spent the next two weeks looking for leftover military equipment, gathering intelligence from government buildings, providing medical care to residents, and getting schools ready for children to return. It really felt like our war was over. We did all that we'd been sent there to do and did it quickly and professionally.

Not long after this President Bush declared our mission accomplished, and we began to work our way south so that we could make the return trip home. Everyone knew that there would be some friction as we helped the country get back on its feet and reestablish a viable government, but we believed the hard work was done.

Several weeks passed, but eventually we made our way back to Kuwait, where we boarded airplanes bound for March Air Reserve Base in Southern California. The flight back home was the strangest flight of my life. We flew on a commercial airline with a flight crew who told us they had volunteered to pick us up and take us home. Unlike other flights I had been on, none of the normal rules applied. We were treated like heroes by pilots and flight attendants and could have done just about anything we wanted to on that plane short of opening a door in-flight.

When we finally landed in California, there were fire trucks on the runway with sirens blaring, shooting their water cannons in the air to celebrate our arrival. A crowd was gathered at the fence of the runway, holding signs and cheering for us as we left the plane, and the USO had set up a holding area where we would get on buses for home with everything we would need to pass the time. Finally, we disembarked the buses that had taken us back to Camp Pendleton and marched in formation to a crowd of loved ones, media, and other appreciative Americans. It was an incredible time, to say the least.

The next several weeks were spent attending memorial services to honor those who had given their lives in Iraq, turning in gear, and getting the battalion ready for a new command and the many new Marines just graduating from the School of Infantry. I was busy checking out as I prepared for a new phase of life outside the Marine Corps, joined in this process by many of the more senior Marines with whom I had served. We had done something important—we defeated the enemy, we won the war, and now we were going to move on.

It's almost funny to look back and realize just how wrong we were. Less than a year later many of those young Marines in the Battalion would find themselves back in Iraq in one of the most difficult urban battles in history, the first battle of Fallujah. And it would not, of course, end there. As this is being written, the United States has been in conflict in Iraq for fifteen years. The numbers have changed and the strategy has changed, but the war is still raging. We may have felt like it was over, but someone apparently forgot to tell the bad guys, and unfortunately, the enemy does get a vote in just how long these things last.

It is not my intent to deal with the politics or execution of the war over the last fifteen years or even to give an opinion as to how a peace that we fought so hard to obtain was lost and how the country spiraled out of control. There is, however, a very important lesson that can be learned from this for anyone dealing with loss or difficulty.

Eventually, if you are willing to work and to wait patiently, you will get to the other side of this trial. You will fight and struggle until it feels like the war is finally over. And this is where so many fail. We move past the current crisis and are so happy that we have, that we set ourselves up for another one. We stop fighting and give up on whatever moved us beyond the last struggle. We can win the battles, but we need to be careful not to mistake this for winning the war. There will always be an enemy waiting for the situation to change or for us to let our guard down so that they can take back the ground they lost.

The crazy thing about this is that the next fight may not necessarily look like the last, which is often the reason it's so unexpected. The war continues but not only in the physical, force-against-force way that we can see. For many who have served in combat in one of the theaters of war over the last seventy years, life didn't get difficult until they came home. More veterans have killed themselves over the last fifteen years than have been killed by the enemy. Divorce rates among those who have served are incredibly high, and diagnosis of mental and emotional disorders has almost become an expected part of military service. When those who serve return home, it feels like the war has come to an end, but for many it is just beginning.

As a Christian, I believe in the ultimate victory that will be realized for those who are in Christ Jesus. I understand, however, that until that day, we will either fight or be overwhelmed by the battles of life. We need to march every day, even when coming out of a battle, or the next one may kill us. How we handle victory may be more important than how we handle loss.

So how do we march when we feel like we've gotten to the other side of a trial?

DON'T FORGET WHERE YOU CAME FROM.

As we were getting ready to deploy to Kuwait and then while we were in Kuwait waiting to push across the border into Iraq, we received several classes on the history, culture, and people living in this region and in the country of Iraq. We were taught quite a few things I don't remember, but one of the things that struck me at the time, something I still use to frame my understanding of what is happening there today, is the fact that Iraq not only boasts the oldest civilization on earth, but is a country defined through history by foreign occupation, regional conflict, and the governing of local warlords.

Iraq has had brief periods of peace throughout its history but is mainly characterized by turmoil and unrest. It was always interesting to talk to the folks who lived on the many farms and in the villages of Iraq, most of whom were grateful for any help they could get. It was hard for me to get over the fact that such a large population allowed themselves to be terrorized by a relatively small group of leaders. This is puzzling until you realize that this is their history. The population of Iraq and of many other countries accept conflict and even violence as a part of life. This is how it's been for thousands of years. Although the people are happy during the periods of peace, they do not expect them to last.

Americans assume that everyone wants the same level of peace and stability that we enjoy and find it hard to believe that someone would not. We also assume that when the fighting stops, the political and cultural environment will change. For those who live in Iraq, peace is just the interlude between conflicts. Again, I'm not rendering an opinion on why we haven't been able to get control in Iraq, but I do believe that, at least in part, we forgot how we got there in the first place. We believed that we could change thousands of years of history and culture in a few months and because of this set ourselves up for the next conflict.

If we forget how we ended up in our battles, we are going to repeat the decisions and behaviors that led us there to begin with. We may find ourselves in a moment of peace, but if we aren't careful, what feels like peace will just be the interlude between conflicts. There will always be battles, but we don't have to fight the same battles again and again if we are willing to learn the lessons of the past. Remember the decisions and behaviors that dragged you into the fight in the first place, and those trials can be an opportunity to grow instead of events to be repeated.

DON'T FORGET WHAT IT TOOK TO GET YOU HERE.

On the other side of the *don't forget where you came from* coin is remembering what you had to do to win. What decisions did you need to make, what behaviors did you have to change, and what disciplines did you have to embrace to win the battles that have been won in your life? Most of the time we do not win without taking deliberate steps to do so. Recognizing that we are in a fight is one thing; understanding what needs to be done to get out is something entirely different.

It has been an honor over the last several years to work with veterans and active-duty service members dealing with trauma related to combat and military service. I've enjoyed helping these men and women understand that a traumatic event, whether it came in combat or life, does not need to define who they are. They need to understand that they were created to live lives of hope and purpose and move forward despite their past.

One of the things we try to convey when teaching or doing one-on-one counseling is that they have already demonstrated that they know how to fight and win. The people who come through our Mighty Oaks Programs are men and women who were taught how to fight a real enemy and have done it. It is extremely important that we emphasize this truth because as they deal with a different fight at home, they are going to need to apply the same effort and many of the same principles to win.

Life after the military has brought a different set of battles, but the lessons learned through military service and in combat can be used to overcome and move forward. Most of us, whether we have served in the military or not, have had to deal with difficulty and overcome obstacles in the past. For those who met the challenge of those times and persevered through them, there were lessons learned that can be applied to the new battles they now must face.

Those who learn how to deal with tragedy or trial are those who understand how to march when others stay where they are and die! They've learned the same skills and tools that need to be utilized when the next battle comes, as it inevitably will. Don't forget what it took to get you here and don't forget the lessons learned in the battles of the past. Trials can be a time of personal growth if we don't forget what it takes to get to the other side of them.

NEVER STOP FIGHTING.

This is probably the most important step of all. Make a decision that you will never stop fighting. Don't ever give up. Don't ever decide that the last fight was your last fight and that now is the time to roll over and die. Understanding that there really is no such thing as a final victory can be discouraging if we think that the goal of life is to live without trials or difficulties.

While no one wants to live their entire life in one big battle, we do need to understand that life is made up of both the good times and the bad, the trials and the victories. Often the greatest meaning in life is found when we work through an overwhelming situation and come out on the other side with the skills necessary to help others fight their fights. Understanding that there will always be another battle to fight doesn't have to be discouraging, but it should keep us from being surprised when that battle does come. It should cause us to decide before the next storm that we are not going to give up.

Before September 11, 2001, the United States experienced a long period of relative peace. Except for Somalia and Desert Storm, we had not been involved in a large-scale conflict since the Vietnam War. For those of us who trained to fight America's next war, that meant that we needed to hear from those who had experienced Vietnam, Somalia and Desert Storm. We would attend lectures from the veterans of these wars and read books written by those who had been there. We would perform training exercises based on battles from these conflicts and try to learn from them in the relative safety of a training environment.

It was because of the lessons learned by others in battles fought around the world that we were able to accomplish many of the things we did. They fought and won so that we could fight and win. The wars in Iraq and Afghanistan have now gone on so long that the generation of men and women who were new to the military when they began are now teaching those who were small children in 2001. They are using the lessons they've learned from battles fought and won to make sure a new generation of warfighters can also fight and win.

It may be that the battle you are fighting today will be the difference between winning and losing for someone else in the future. Maybe it's just the next step in your growth as a person maturing through the various stages of life. Whatever the case, you will never learn or grow if you decide that it's just easier to quit. Never stop fighting, and you will be prepared for whatever comes next.

CONCLUSION

There is something comforting in believing that the fight we are in right now will be our last. We are motivated to figure it out and get to the other side of this conflict, hoping that we will never have to deal with it again. Although I've known some people who seem to enjoy conflict, most of us really do want to live lives of peace. Hopefully you will not have to fight the same fight again, and hopefully you will learn the lessons that you need to learn and move on. The reality, though, is that even if you never fight this fight again, there will be another one that demands your attention.

But this truth does not have to be discouraging. It should equip you with a mindset that allows you to experience victory in all the battles of life and not just in the one that you are facing now. It's amazing the lessons that can be learned when we look at our trials as an opportunity to learn instead of situations to avoid. My purpose in writing this book is exactly that. Iraq was an opportunity for me to learn life lessons that have in many ways carried me forward. I don't ever want to waste a hardship or trial by failing to learn from it.

Life involves both ups and downs. Those who are the most productive and contribute the most to the people who come into their lives are the ones who keep fighting, keep learning, and keep winning. Decide today that regardless of what may happen in the future, you will never quit. You have the skills and the experience you need to win. You have learned the lessons that will get you through. Take the lessons, apply them to your life, and confidently move forward.

DON'T STOP FIGHTING.

- *Don't forget where you came from.*
- *Don't forget what it took to get you here.*
- Never stop fighting.

CHAPTER 15 - UNDERSTAND THAT GOD IS SOVEREIGN

Have you ever asked yourself why you become overwhelmed, frustrated, and depressed when life doesn't go according to plan? We get so upset about what others are doing or about the circumstances in our lives, but I'm not sure we ever really ask *why* we are upset.

It's easy to say, "I'm upset because my relationships, finances, or plans for the future are falling apart. I'm depressed because I've lost someone I care for deeply or because I've been told that my health isn't good." Any of those are reasons for sadness (a normal human response), but sadness is different than becoming angry, overwhelmed with anxiety, or something worse—feeling as if our world is spinning out of control.

When I look at my own life, I believe the key word in all of this is that last word: control. We respond negatively when we feel as though we've lost control or that control is being taken away from us. Most of our lives are invested in controlling our world, and losing control can cause us to live in fear of what *might* happen.

As I mentioned in chapter one, the event on the bridge over the Saddam Canal changed many of the ways I look at life. But the biggest shift in my outlook came when it was over. When the battle was finished and I had time to reflect, it occurred to me that the best I could do was not enough to keep me out of trouble. The enemy did not care where I went to school, who my parents were, or what town I grew up in. They did not care what position I graduated in at Officer Candidates School or the fact that I have a wife and children at home. The fact that I had spent years preparing to lead Marines in combat and learn how to control that environment meant nothing to the people trying to kill me.

While it's true that I need to be prepared and do the very best I can, at the end of the day my confidence must be in a sovereign God. This was a real moment of revelation to me. When I stopped believing that it was all up to me, that I had to be in control to win, I was finally able to experience peace regardless of my situation.

This truth was cemented in my mind during that event on the Saddam Canal, but the thought did not start there. The opening days of the war were difficult, as one might imagine, but more because of the uncertainty of it all than because of the fear often associated with combat. We were well-trained and mentally prepared for what we were doing. But as situations changed and one day blended into the next, that uncertainty, coupled with the fatigue that comes from days without rest, began to take an emotional toll.

It's funny how you can *feel* like you're in danger even when you're not, and that danger is just as real to you as if you were. This was the situation we were in a few days after crossing the border as we sat on a road in the middle of the night, waiting for the order to continue pushing north. As I sat there, the darkness became overwhelming. I'm sure it was the emotion of the previous few days coupled with the exhaustion of not sleeping, but I will never forget how that darkness felt. Sometimes even now if I am outside late at night or early in the morning, that same feeling comes over me and I think back to that day.

With the night closing in I sat and did the only thing I could: I listened to the radio traffic on our battalion frequency. Nothing unusual, for the most part, until an intelligence update was given on a battle we knew was taking place in a town called Nasiriyah. The report said that things weren't going well and several soldiers had been captured. For some reason, hearing that caused the oppressing darkness to turn into fear. It didn't even make sense. We were in no danger, and I sat there surrounded by a battalion of Marines, weapons, and vehicles. The fear did not make sense (fear seldom does), but it was very real.

At that moment a Bible verse came to my mind that I have no recollection of ever memorizing. The verse was from the Old Testament book of Isaiah, chapter 41 verse 10:

> *"Fear thou not, for I am with thee. Be not dismayed, for I am thy God. I will strengthen thee, yea, I will help thee, yea I will uphold thee with the right hand of my righteousness."*

I still don't know when I learned or even heard that verse, but it came to mind at the moment I needed it most, and the overwhelming darkness and fear that was creeping in went away. It was still dark outside, but the emotional darkness that was overwhelming me became peace.

Nothing in my situation had changed. The only thing that had changed was my perspective. Instead of looking at myself as the one who needed to be in control, I realized that God, who is much bigger than me or my circumstances, already was. I will never be strong enough or capable enough or smart enough to bring peace to my world. God, though, is sovereign (He rules over everything), and His desire will ultimately come to pass. Since fear is a human emotion, it's one I've experienced many times since then. But when I can stop long enough to focus on a God who has ultimate control instead of on myself, peace will come *in the storm,* not after it has gone away.

REALIZE THAT THERE WILL ALWAYS BE THINGS YOU DON'T UNDERSTAND.

This may be the most difficult step for those going through a difficult time of life, particularly when they want to believe that God is capable and has a plan. We want to believe that there is a reason for all of it, but we can't figure it out. Before we can find peace when our world is falling apart and it's hard to figure out, we need to accept that there will always be things that we just do not understand.

Many will look to a verse like Romans 8:28 and conclude that someday they will understand. This verse does bring a tremendous amount of comfort: "And we know that all things work together for good to them that love God, to them who are the called according to his purpose." We love this verse because, among other things, it causes us to believe that the picture will all come together someday, and we will be able to step back and say, "Now I get it! It all makes sense."

But that's not what the verse means. Is God bringing everything together, like a giant puzzle, to accomplish His ultimate purpose? Of course! Will we always know what that is? Not necessarily. Isaiah 55:8-9 says it this way: "For my thoughts are not your thoughts, neither are your ways my ways, saith the LORD. For as the heavens are higher than the earth, so are my ways higher than your ways, and my thoughts than your thoughts."

We could also look to that well-known story of Job, a man of character who trusted God but suffered greatly. There was a reason for that suffering, but the reason was never revealed to him. He was to simply remain faithful even when he didn't understand. This can be so hard for us, and I have met many people who stop marching right here. Since they can't understand why, they stop moving forward.

God is no less good when our circumstances don't make sense, but we need to trust Him if we are going to find peace when they don't.

DON'T RELY ON WHAT YOU SEE RIGHT NOW. WHAT YOU SEE NOW IS NOT THE WHOLE PICTURE—GOD SEES THE WHOLE PICTURE.

This is the next part of the last step. We have trouble trusting God because we can only see our small corner of the world, but God is looking at the big picture. There were times in Iraq when I remember getting so angry at the orders we were given. It didn't always make sense to me why we needed to set up a check-point on a particular road or risk the lives of our Marines to go into a village that had very little consequence to the overall mission (as I understood it). We would move all night to get to a point on the map as quickly as possible only to sit at that point for days at a time. Not understanding everything else that was going on, these movements made little sense.

Now, looking back, I can see that much of what didn't make sense to me was necessary so that the other pieces of the puzzle could be put where they belong. At the time, though, I thought that I should have been making more of the decisions! I have heard Marines accuse leadership of not caring about whether the men lived or died because they did not get the support they asked for. It's amazing how everyone in the Marine Corps feels like they could do a better job of planning an operation than those who have been doing it for thirty years!

While I am certain that there are incompetent or incapable leaders at every level, the frustration often felt by those lower on the leadership hierarchy (down near the bottom where I was) is the result of not seeing the big picture. There is quite a bit of arrogance that goes along with believing that with limited information and a very narrow view of the battlefield you know exactly what should be done all the time. And yet I and many others were just that arrogant. Now, we all need to do the best we can with the information and opportunities that we do have (we will talk about that next), but viewing the rest of the world through your very specific and very narrow situation will lead to some dangerous thoughts.

I left the Marine Corps shortly after returning from Iraq. Over the intervening years I have watched documentaries about the invasion, read books about it, and talked to many others who were also there. I have learned far more about the reasons for so many of the decisions made in the last several years than I ever understood while they were being implemented. Multiple countries and a few hundred thousand troops all working together, political concerns as well as a post-war plan, not to mention the sheer logistical burden of making it all happen, and I spent many angry hours worrying about why we were either moving too fast or not fast enough. It seems a little absurd now, but in the moment, anger and frustration made sense.

And that is how it is in life. We talk about a sovereign God who has a plan beyond our ability to understand, but we get upset when we don't understand what we are going through right now. God is looking at a timeline that extends back to eternity past and forward into eternity future. He is concerned for the generations of humans who have and will live. He has put a plan in motion for the redemption of mankind and for His ultimate glory, but we do not have the ability to see or understand it all.

Don't make decisions about God or His ultimate plan based only on the piece that you can see. Trust that there is more to the puzzle and that, maybe not your day but someday, it will all come together.

YOU ARE RESPONSIBLE FOR WHAT YOU CAN CONTROL (BUT ONLY WHAT YOU CAN CONTROL).

Even though I could not grasp the full scope of the war, I was responsible for my part of it. I was responsible for training Marines so that they would be able to accomplish the mission regardless of what that might be. I was responsible for making the best decisions I could regarding the welfare of my unit and for making good tactical decisions when they were mine to make. I was responsible for accurately communicating the information I was given to the individuals who needed it so that they could then make the best decisions possible. There was quite a bit that I could control and was responsible to control, but there was also quite a bit that I could not. The challenge was understanding the difference.

Much of our frustration in life is the result of us trying to control things outside of our control. Either because the decisions are God's to make or because the people we are dealing with don't necessarily see things the way we want them to, there are things we cannot control and things for which we are not responsible. Finding peace in the midst of battle means doing all that you can with the opportunities and resources that you have and letting God and the other people in your life do the same.

This is the opposite of lazy faith, by the way. I have been told by many people over the years that faith is trusting God and sitting still until He tells us to do something different. There is a time to sit still, of course, but God always works through people who work! That is just good stewardship. Use your time, your abilities, your relationships and your influence to do all that is set in front of you, but be careful to recognize the things that are not yours to control.

PEACE IS FOUND IN THE STORM, NOT AFTER IT.

How often we pray that God would take the trials of life away when, really, we should pray that He will provide peace whether the trial goes away or not. Peace is found in the storm, not after it!

I remember hearing a story years ago that was intended to illustrate this idea of peace. The story, as I remember it, was of a painting contest, the topic of which was peace. The goal was for each of the artists to paint their ideal image of peace, and a panel of judges would decide which one best captured the concept.

When the artists came back on the day their work would be

judged, there were many beautiful paintings depicting some of the most peaceful scenes imaginable. There were paintings of pastures and sunsets and of children playing and animals grazing. The painting that won the contest, though, surprised everyone. The winning painting depicted a small boat on a stormy sea. The sky was black and ominous, and the rain was torrential. The wind was strong, depicted by waves crashing over the boat. The picture appeared to be the opposite of a peaceful scene until a final detail jumped out. Even though there was chaos going on outside of the boat, there was a small bird sleeping soundly inside, protected from the storm by a small ledge designed to keep the water out. Peace for this bird was not found apart from the storm. Peace was found in spite of the storm.

This is exactly how we must view peace. If we are seeking refuge in the right place, there is not a storm or trial that can destroy us. The Bible says it this way in Psalm 91:1: "He that dwelleth in the secret place of the most High shall abide under the shadow of the Almighty. I will say of the LORD, He is my refuge and my fortress: my God; in Him will I trust."

When your world feels like it's falling apart, don't pray for deliverance so that you can experience peace. Trust in the One who gives peace as the storms rage around you.

DEAL WITH FEAR AND MOVE ON.

Being afraid is not always something you can control. How you deal with that fear, however, is. As John Wayne once said (or at least what they quote him as saying on coffee cups and plaques), "Courage is being afraid and saddling up anyway." That may not seem very deep, but it's true. Faith in God is not the absence of fear or apprehension. It is being afraid but trusting Him more.

As I sat in the dark with fear coming over me, listening to events unfold several miles away, the verse that came to mind told me not to fear because I could trust God to hold me! Because God is bigger than the things that were bringing the fear, I could move forward despite it.

If you are going to move forward, if you are going to march when all you want to do is lay down and die, you need to recognize fear, look to a sovereign God in faith, and take the next step. So many people quit simply because they fear what might happen. What *might* happen is not ours to control. We simply need to keep moving forward.

CONCLUSION

The sovereignty of God is a topic I will never fully understand. There are many gifted theologians and Bible scholars who have spent the better part of their lives preaching and writing on this specific aspect of God's character. So much of this work helps to put into perspective just how big God is and how small we are. I am thankful to know that He has a plan and the power to bring that plan together. He is sovereign—He rules over everything, and I do not. That is a good thing to know.

I have often struggled with the concept of God's sovereignty from a practical standpoint. I know that He is sovereign. That is a truth. I do not dispute it or deny it. When I read so much of what has been written on it, however, I am left feeling that because He is sovereign, I need to just hang on knowing that everything will work out in the end.

It is easy to lose hope for a productive life or victory in storms if we believe that God's sovereignty removes our ability to make decisions that impact our lives. It is easy to come to a place where, instead of moving forward when the mortar rounds of life begin to fall, we stay where we are and hope that God will move us if it is within the scope of His sovereign will. We die in place and blame God—in righteous-sounding language, of course—for our death.

Blaming others in our lives for our circumstances can absolutely destroy our ability to move forward. How sad it is when, instead of blaming others, we blame God by refusing to get up when we are down or move forward when we are under attack because, "God is sovereign and will move me if He wants me moved."

The sovereignty of God is not something that should remove the hope of a productive life. God's sovereignty should not remove the belief that we can make decisions that will impact the outcome of our storms. Sovereignty brings great hope and encouragement because we understand that God is in control and has a plan and that we don't need to worry about how it all comes together. We find hope and peace when we realize that we are responsible for the decisions we make about the things we can control, and not responsible for the rest! We are the best stewards we can be of the resources and opportunities that God has placed into our hands while trusting Him.

As I led my small group of Marines in Iraq, I often spent so much time worrying or upset about the decisions being made outside of my control that I missed the opportunities that were within it. I lacked peace because, instead of focusing on what was mine to affect, I focused on so much that was not.

Peace comes when we learn to take our eyes off our circumstances, abilities, and opportunities, or the lack thereof, and begin to trust a God who is bigger and has a plan beyond what we can see. We do what is within our control, we steward what He has given, and we leave the rest to Him. That is peace. Not peace beyond the storm, but peace in the storm.

God is big. God has a plan. God is sovereign. Do all that you can. Trust Him!

UNDERSTAND THAT GOD IS SOVEREIGN.

- *Realize that there will always be things you don't understand.*
- *Don't rely on what you see right now. What you see now is not the whole picture—God sees the whole picture.*
- *You are responsible for what you can control (but only what you can control).*
- *Peace is found in the storm, not after it.*
- *Deal with fear and move on.*

CHAPTER 16 - DECIDE: YOU WILL TAKE THE MOUNTAIN

Winning begins with a decision. Until we make the decision to press on to the end, we are not prepared for what we will inevitably face. No one knows everything that will happen in the future, but if the past teaches us anything, it's that the good things we enjoy will be offset by times of difficulty.

Storms and battles are a normal part of life, but so many of us are ill-prepared when they come. We face unexpected hardship and respond as if hardship of any kind is completely unexpected. Then we try to figure out what we're going to do. Since we either did not expect this trial or hoped that it would never come, we begin to evaluate whether we want to stick it out. We quit on important relationships, walk away from jobs, or, worse yet, stop living a life of faith because it's just too hard. There may be a reward on the other side of each of those, but when the storm comes, we decide that it's just not worth it.

How often we later regret walking away when we should have walked forward. The key is not waiting until the trial comes to decide what we are going to do. We need to decide that no matter what happens, we will not quit. Life will have times of difficulty, but the greatest victories come to those who persevere.

In Joshua 14:6 we find the end of Caleb's story, and what a great ending it is. In his eighties, Caleb finally stood in the land promised by God and let everyone know which part of the Promised Land belonged to him. When he came to the place called Hebron, he declared, "God gave this land to me and now I want this mountain!" For more than forty years Caleb had been hanging on to God's promise because he knew that God would do what He said and that he, Caleb, would live to see that promise fulfilled.

One of the crazy parts of this story is that even though Caleb did finally make it to the land, he still had to fight to make it his. We are told that this eighty-five-year-old man fought the inhabitants of Hebron, kicked them off "his mountain," and began to prepare a place for his family. We get hurt if God does not remove every obstacle in our path, but Caleb was just happy he finally got to fight to accept God's gift! The Bible passage that records this story is a little long, but worth reading:

> *"Then the children of Judah came unto Joshua in Gilgal: and Caleb the son of Jephunneh the Kenezite said unto him, Thou knowest the thing that the LORD said unto Moses the man of God concerning me and thee in Kadeshbarnea. Forty years old was I when Moses the servant of the LORD sent me from Kadeshbarnea to espy out the land; and I brought him word again as it was in mine heart. Nevertheless my brethren that went up with me made the heart of the people melt: but I wholly followed the LORD my God. And Moses sware on that day, saying, Surely the land whereon thy feet have trodden shall be thine inheritance, and thy children's for ever, because thou hast wholly followed the LORD my God. 10 And now, behold, the*

LORD hath kept me alive, as he said, these forty and five years, even since the LORD spake this word unto Moses, while the children of Israel wandered in the wilderness: and now, lo, I am this day fourscore and five years old. As yet I am as strong this day as I was in the day that Moses sent me: as my strength was then, even so is my strength now, for war, both to go out, and to come in.

Now therefore give me this mountain, whereof the LORD spake in that day; for thou heardest in that day how the Anakims were there, and that the cities were great and fenced: if so be the LORD will be with me, then I shall be able to drive them out, as the LORD said.

And Joshua blessed him, and gave unto Caleb the son of Jephunneh Hebron for an inheritance.

Hebron therefore became the inheritance of Caleb the son of Jephunneh the Kenezite unto this day, because that he wholly followed the LORD God of Israel. And the name of Hebron before was Kirjatharba; which Arba was a great man among the Anakims. And the land had rest from war."

- Joshua 14:6-15

By all indications, Caleb was a good man. He loved and honored God, took care of his family, and was faithful to do the things he needed to do. But even with that, Caleb had to endure forty years of heartache, disappointment, and loss. But he came out on the other side because he never let the difficult things keep him from doing right.

As you read the above passage you see again and again that Caleb talks about "wholly following God." The land was his, and he had something of value to leave to his family because he decided that regardless of how difficult life became, he would just keep pressing on. Caleb saw the promise of God fulfilled in his life because he refused to give up in the storm. He made a decision to march when he could have stayed where he was and died.

I love the story of Caleb because it so clearly demonstrates what a life of following God should look like. A decision was made to do right, which, instead of accolades, brought rejection, hardship, a long walk, and a big fight. But because he was willing to take one day at a time, always trusting that the ultimate outcome would be exactly as God said it would be, he saw God do the miraculous.

I love this because for a person who wants to follow God, this life can be discouraging. While I would like to say that I never ask the question, "Is it worth it," I often do. What we need to realize in these difficult times, though, is that it is always worth it. That the pursuit of God is the reason we were created and that as we pursue Him, He will bless our lives. As followers of God we need to understand that we are not walking and fighting for the victory; we are walking and fighting because the victory has already been secured.

Don't quit. Never give up. Decide that regardless of what may happen in your life you will not stop until you claim your mountain!

"O death, where is thy sting? O grave, where is thy victory?
The sting of death is sin; and the strength of sin is the law.
But thanks be to God, which giveth us the victory through
our Lord Jesus Christ. Therefore, my beloved brethren, be ye
stedfast, unmoveable, always abounding in the work of the Lord,
forasmuch as ye know that your labour is not in vain in the Lord.

- I Corinthians 15:55-58

"And let us not be weary in well doing: for in due season we
shall reap, if we faint not."

- Galatians 6:9

CONCLUSION

It's interesting how your perspective can change as you get older. Concepts and ideas that you thought you understood look completely different through the lens of time and experience. One of these areas for me where my perspective has changed and my understanding has evolved is related to the concept of heroism.

I remember when I was young watching movies where the hero was the strongest, toughest and smartest guy around. He would do things that others lacked the courage to even attempt because his physical and intellectual ability set him apart from everyone else. In a way I think it was many of these characters who initially pushed me toward military service. I wanted to be a hero and thought that the most heroic people in the world were those who served in the military (particularly the Marines, which I still kind of believe). To me, and to most young boys, there was just something different about those who were willing to fight a nation's battles so that the rest of the nation didn't have to.

Those who serve are still my heroes, but not for the same reason as when I was young. I used to think that these warriors were different than everyone else. That they were stronger and smarter and had some grasp on courage that others just couldn't understand. But then I got to know people who have served and who are still serving. I have met those in the military who are stronger and smarter than most, but I have also met many who are pretty average. There are those who are college educated and others who aren't. There are those from families with a strong military heritage and some who are the first person in their family to put on a uniform. Some from good homes and some from not so good homes. Those who serve, at least from my experience, reflect the rest of the world. By the time I became a Marine, I had already figured this truth out, but the realization was a bit disillusioning. These men and women are heroes, but if they are just like everyone else, what makes them special? Why do we honor and respect them and thank them for their service?

There are nearly four-hundred million people living in the United States right now, but the veteran population stands at somewhere around twenty-three million. That means that if I have done my math correctly, veterans from every war since World War II represent around one-half of one percent of the population. Less than half of a percent have, at some point in their lives, promised to defend the Constitution of the United States and the American way of life. We honor those who have served or are serving in the military not because they are intrinsically more valuable than someone else but because they have been willing to do what most other would not. They are heroes because they are have stood in the gap, offering their lives so that we can be free. And this is heroism—doing what must be done for people who are either unwilling or unable to do it themselves. It is the essence of selfless devotion to duty.

As my understanding of this concept has become clearer over the years I've begun to see that heroism, doing what must be done for others who are either unwilling or unable to do it themselves, is an everyday occurrence. Not just in the military, but everywhere someone is willing to do what is right for the good of others even when the personal cost is more than most others are willing to pay. The dad who goes to work every day for his family and does all that he can to take care of them is a hero. The single mom working two jobs while raising her kids to do something important with their lives is a hero. The person who works for less pay because it gives them the opportunity to volunteer and help those who cannot help themselves is a hero. The family ministering to the underprivileged in a country far from home are heroes. These heroes may not get recognition or have others thank them for their service, but they are heroes nonetheless because they have decided to fight the battles that most are unwilling to fight. Heroes are those who understand that life will always involve a fight but that there is a reward for those who are willing to push forward when others quit.

It is not just those who wear a uniform who need to know how to fight. All of us will have to fight if we want to live a life of value. If we want to have marriages, relationships with our children, and friendships and careers that are meaningful, we must get up every time we fall. We need to recognize when the enemy attacks and make an active decision that we will not lay there and die, but will march forward, refusing to give up.

The battles will come—you can't control that—but no one can take away your ability to act when it does. So what are you going to do? Breathing is not the same thing as living. Those who truly live understand that life is often hard but that nothing in this life can remove your decision to move forward in a meaningful, hope-filled way.

Are you living or are you simply hanging on until your body gives up? You were created for more and can achieve more if only you will. When the mortar rounds of life begin to fall on your position, you really only have two choices: decide to stay where you are and die, or decide to get up, march forward, and live the life you were created to live.

March or die—the choice is yours.

FINAL THOUGHTS

WHY IS LIFE SO HARD?

Any discussion of overcoming life's battles must include a discussion around the question, "Why?" Why is life so hard? This is a question that has probably been asked since the beginning of human history (although the first humans could just look at each other and know why). It takes forms like:

"Why do good things happen to bad people?"

"Why is there evil in the world?"

"Why do the innocent suffer?"

"Where does discrimination come from?"

"If God is just, why is there so much injustice?"

For some reason we would rather discuss why things are so difficult instead of asking how we can deal with the difficulty. Maybe it's easier to talk about why, or maybe it just makes us feel better when we can come up with an answer. If we can answer the why question, then we can rationalize the pain and suffering in our lives and in the lives of those we care about. If we can explain it, it doesn't hurt as much.

The problem with asking why is that there isn't always a satisfactory answer. We try to figure it out, and when we can't, we become bitter or depressed at best or simply give up at worst. I have spoken to people who talk about how they "lost their faith" or can't believe because there is so much difficulty in the world. They explain that not being able to answer the why question in a way that makes sense to them has brought hopelessness about their future and a lack of motivation to go on. Still others, concluding that there is no reason for the challenges they endure other than chance, live their lives in the pursuit of comfort and pleasure. They avoid pain, at least to the extent that they can, and fill their lives with things of passing value.

Either way, not understanding why can cause major problems in a world where there will always be problems. So even though not every question can be answered, this is where we must begin.

So why is life so difficult? Why do we have to fight to overcome these difficulties and live the life that we were created to live? Where does our enemy, the one we are fighting against, come from? Since there are several very large books written by people smarter than I on the origin and operation of trial and difficulty in our world, I will keep it short and simple. This is not exhaustive, but provides some context as we move forward.

WHY IS LIFE SO DIFFICULT?

When discussing the topic of difficulty or trial in life it is important that we begin at the beginning. Thanks to the Bible, we know that a life of hardship was never part of the plan. If we open the Bible to Genesis 1, we see that God created the earth, the animals, and men to live in perfect harmony with one another and in perfect fellowship with Him. We don't know how long this perfect situation lasted (as described in Genesis 1-2), but we do know that because of a decision by the first man and woman to sin, it eventually ended.

What is sin? Sin, simply put, is rebellion against the plan and person of God. It is falling short of His standard of perfection by willfully walking away from His purpose. God, who created man to have a relationship with him, made it possible for man to decide to walk away from that relationship.

And that is exactly what happened. Adam and Eve exercised their free will, doing the one thing God told them not to do. The sin was not about eating fruit; it was about rebelling against the word of their Creator. God didn't want to have a relationship based on man's inability to do something else. He wanted to have a relationship based on love and the decision of man to be in that relationship. God, because He is God, understands that even in a perfect environment removing choice or free will turns that environment into a prison instead of something to be enjoyed. But, as with every decision in life, the decision to walk away from God came with consequences.

In Genesis 3 the consequences of Adam and Eve's decision to turn their backs on God are given. We are told that because of this sin, life would become very difficult. There would be times, in fact, when nature itself would fight against humanity. Growing food would become laborious as the ground hardened and the thorns and weeds grew. Childbirth would now take the giver of life, the mother, to the edge of death. The devil, the one who provided the temptation that Adam and Eve pursued, would continue to tempt mankind until the day that he was finally defeated. The greatest consequence of this sin, though, was that in sinning Adam and Eve brought death to the world. Genesis 3:19 says it this way: "In the sweat of thy face shalt thou eat bread, till thou return unto the ground; for out of it wast thou taken: for dust thou art, and unto dust shalt thou return."

Death was a new concept to Adam and Eve. Before sin there was no corruption, and without corruption there was no death. But now that sin was present, everything living had begun the slow process of dying. This death was not only physical, however. The death brought on by sin included the physical, but death of the soul was now the reality. In Romans 6:23 we learn that "the wages of sin is death." The penalty or payment for sin, what is deserved for sin, is death. While physical death is a final step for the body, spiritual death is an eternal separation from God! It is a soul-level brokenness that separates us from the perfect relationship that God designed and causes that brokenness to infect all of life.

Thankfully, there is a path to restoration of our relationship with God which will be discussed in the next chapter. The consequence of sin and brokenness, however, is something that will overshadow all of life until ultimate victory is gained by God Himself. There are wars between nations, deep hurt in relationships, and evils of all kind committed in every community in the world because soul-brokenness perverts our view of truth and causes us to engage in entirely self-centered pursuits. There can be restoration of soul for the individual, but even those restored in a relationship with their Creator through Christ will have to deal with the consequences of their own sin and the sin of those around them. Life is hard because we as people are dealing with the consequence of a race (the human race) that has willfully stepped out of the Creator's plan for their lives.

This is the point where many will say something like this: "That's not fair! Why should I be punished for someone else's rebellion against God?" While that sounds like a strong, intellectually grounded question, the Bible puts it another way.

Romans 5:12 says this: "Wherefore, as by one man sin entered into the world, and death by sin; and so death passed upon all men, for that all have sinned." This verse brings the discussion of why we must deal with the consequences of sin (the reason life is so difficult) to an interesting point. Why do we have to deal with this?

1. The sin of others.

   Since the creation of man humans have had to deal with the sin of Adam. He was the first man and when he sinned he, by virtue of being our common father, sinned for all of us. Again, it does not seem fair that this is the case, but truth does not change because we don't like it. It is not difficult to see, however, that since the beginning humans have sinned. There was murder in the first family (Genesis 4) and in every generation since that time. Often, what we deal with in this world is the consequence of someone else's decision to violate God's perfect plan and to go their own way. Sin and brokenness exist around us even if we are not actively participating.

2.   Our own sin.

The second reason we deal with the consequences of sin, as given in this verse, is because we are all sinners! I love the way the Bible deals with this topic because there is no ambiguity. The author of Romans, where this verse is found, is a preacher. He is an Apostle named Paul. As I read this verse I can almost hear Paul, who I am sure had encountered every objection to this concept of sin, saying something like, "Let me make this very clear: everyone here is a sinner! You may think that you are better than someone else or that it is not fair that you must deal with the consequences of someone else's sin. What you must understand is that your sin is just as bad as everyone else's and causes damage to your relationship with God, your relationship with others, and the way you live in this world." He wanted his listeners and readers to make this matter of sin a personal one.

I believe that all of us, if we are being honest, know that we willfully rebel against God's plan for our lives. Perhaps not all of the time, but we struggle with pursuing His path or pursuing ours. There is harmony when His path becomes ours, but chaos and friction when it is not. Not following God's plan is sin. And there are consequences.

In this life we deal with the consequences of the sin of others as well as the consequences of our own. We don't like it, but the truth remains. Thankfully, we can be restored in our relationship with God (again, that will be discussed in the next chapter), but until final restoration comes by way of the return of Christ, there will be brokenness, pain, and hardship.

ARE THERE ANY OTHER REASONS FOR HARDSHIP IN LIFE?

A fair question to ask at this point is, "Are there any non-sin, non-rebellion related reasons for difficulty in life?" That is a fair question because we know that not everything that makes life hard to live is the direct result of sin. It is sin that brought the corruption of body and mind that will often cause our body to fail and our mind to make bad decisions, but it is not necessarily rebellion against God that brings pain into our lives. The decision that I made as a platoon commander in the fire-fight at the Saddam Canal to stop on top of the bridge was not a good decision. Fortunately, we were able to deal with my bad decision, but we also had to deal with some very real consequences. Now, I didn't do that because I was willfully disobeying God. I was not trying to rebel against His plan or pursue my own path instead of His. I simply made a decision based on what I knew at the moment. It was not a great decision, but it wasn't sin either. My brain does not work at full capacity because of the physical corruption that is the result of sin, but a bad decision made with a brain that doesn't function at capacity is not always sinful. This is the reason we expect children to make bad decisions understanding they are not necessarily trying to be rebellious. Their brains don't function at full capacity, so there will be times they do things that are harmful, but not sinful.

Here is the point: there are difficult and often overwhelming circumstances in life that come about because of a sincere bad decision or a body that just doesn't work the way it was intended. Are these a consequence of sin? They are a consequence of the corruption in our world because of sin, but they do not necessarily follow sinful behavior. So how do we reconcile these two?

Paul the Apostle, the pastor that we mentioned earlier, was teaching the church in the city of Corinth in I Corinthians 11. In verse 28 of that chapter he uses an interesting phrase: "Let a man examine himself." He was teaching on an ordinance of the church and wanted the folks he was speaking to to make sure they were living the life God wanted them to live. He wanted them to compare the way they were living to the way that God told them to live and then to align themselves with God in any areas where they were not right.

When experiencing difficulty in our lives it is important for us to go through this same process, to examine the way we're living based on the direction we are given in the Bible, God's plan for our lives, and to adjust where necessary. We may need to ask forgiveness from God or others for sin and hurt committed, or we may conclude that the current hardship in our life is not the result of our own sin or walking away from God. We examine our lives against the truth of the Bible and allow God to show us the truth we need in our lives at that time.

We are told in I Peter 4:12, "Beloved, think it not strange

concerning the fiery trial which is to try you, as though some strange thing happened unto you: But rejoice, inasmuch as ye are partakers of Christ's sufferings; that, when his glory shall be revealed, ye may be glad also with exceeding joy."

There will always be difficulty in life. We cannot get away from it. We experience difficulty and brokenness and corruption ultimately because of sin. The sin of others as well as our own has consequences that we cannot escape. Not all difficulty is the direct result of a sinful action, though. Sometimes trials come because we live in a fallen world, even though we are doing the best we can to follow God and His plan for our lives.

When trials and difficulties do come, stop and examine your life. Contrast how you are living with the plan for life given to us in the Bible. Change where change is necessary. Ask forgiveness where that is needed. Learn from bad decisions, yours and others, and decide to move forward. We don't get to decide whether or not there are trials in our lives. We simply get to decide what we will do when they come. Decide to get up and march!

A RELATIONSHIP WITH THE CREATOR

"Therefore if any man be in Christ, he is a new creature: old things are passed away; behold, all things are become new."

- I Corinthians 5:17

Many of you already have a relationship with God through His Son Jesus Christ. You have experienced the forgiveness of sins and the new life found when we surrender to the will of our Creator. It is an amazing thing to know that the One who created the universe and all it contains would desire to have a personal relationship with each one of us. Followers of Christ are far from perfect, but they have the ability to recognize their imperfection and rest in the One who gives them life. To be fully what we were created to be is not possible without this personal relationship.

Others reading this have not yet entered into that personal relationship. For one reason or another you have not accepted that you can or should align yourself with God's eternal purpose for you. There are many reasons that people do not accept this gift. If you are reading this, you are clearly not averse to the Christian worldview. Perhaps you've been hurt or disillusioned by the behavior of those who call themselves Christians or are simply and honestly trying to make the best decision. Whatever the case, I cannot end this book without telling you how to have that relationship.

God created us to be perfect. There was no brokenness in the beginning, and we were in complete communion with Him. We are even told in the third chapter of Genesis that God would personally spend time each evening with the first humans. But then mankind, through our common father Adam, decided to rebel against God's will and do what He had expressly told them not to do. This disobedience (what we call sin) broke our perfect relationship with God and made it impossible for man to walk in communion with Him. Because of sin, this broken relationship carries with it a penalty—separation from God forever in a place called Hell. Certainly not something we like to talk about, but a reality that we all must face.

The great light in this dark story is that God still wants to have a relationship with us and has made that possible through His Son, Jesus Christ. By accepting His gift of forgiveness of sins, each of us can be forgiven and given a new life through Him. Our relationship and communion with the Creator will be restored, and our life will be in line with His purpose.

Having a relationship with Christ and experiencing forgiveness of sins is not some formulaic process but rather an acceptance of a gift freely offered to us by Him. Some thoughts for those who would like to enter into that relationship:

1. Recognize your condition.

    To find the way to eternal life with God, you must admit that you are lost in sin. Romans 5:12 teaches us that since Adam and Eve, the first man and woman on earth, a sin nature has been present in all people. Romans 3:23 says, *"For all have sinned, and come short of the glory of God."* Sin is any act contrary to God's laws and commandments, and the sins you have committed separate you from God.

Sin has a penalty. Romans 6:23 says, *"For the wages of sin is death; but the gift of God is eternal life through Jesus Christ our Lord."* The wage or payment for our sin is spiritual death and eternal separation from God.

2. Realize that religion and good works are not the answer.

    Religions try to create their own ways to God. Their systems may seem logical, but they cannot bridge the gap created by our sin. Proverbs 14:12 says, *"There is a way which seemeth right unto a man, but the end thereof are the ways of death."* In other words, our thoughts and ways are not what matter.

    God's Word, the Bible, provides true answers of grace and forgiveness. The Bible says in Ephesians 2:8–9, *"For by grace are ye saved through faith; and that not of ourselves: it is the gift of God: Not of works, lest any man should boast."*

3. The good news is that Jesus has made a way!

    Even though we were lost and separated from God, He loved us.

Because of that love, God sent His Son to die on the cross and raised him from the dead three days later. John 3:16 explains, *"For God so loved the world, that he gave his only begotten Son, that whosoever believeth in him should not perish, but have everlasting life."* Through the death and resurrection of Jesus, He became the payment for our sin. Now we don't have to pay for our sin ourselves. By His grace, salvation is provided. Romans 5:8 says, *"But God commendeth [meaning proved or demonstrated] his love toward us, in that, while we were yet sinners, Christ died for us."*

4. Believe and receive Christ.

To have a relationship with God and an eternal home in Heaven, we must stop trusting ourselves, our works, and our religions, and place our full trust in Jesus Christ alone for the forgiveness of our sin and eternal life. Roman 10:13 says, *"For whosoever shall call upon the name of the Lord shall be saved."* That is a promise directly from God that if you will pray to Him, confess that you are a sinner, ask Him to forgive your sins, and turn to Him alone to be your Savior, He promises to save you and give you the free gift of eternal life.

You can make that decision by praying to Him today. There are no magic words and no magic prayers. God simply desires to hear you express an understanding of your need for Him and your desire to have a relationship with Him.

My prayer is that if you have not yet entered into that relationship, today is the day you accept His gift of salvation and begin living in relationship with your Creator.